Living in the Black

Brenda Blackmon
Alyssa Curry

Living in the Black
Copyright © 2014
Brenda Blackmon and Alyssa Curry

All rights reserved. Printed and bound in the United State of America. No part of this book may be reproduced or transmitted in any form by any means, electric or mechanical, including photocopying, recording, or by an information storage and retrieval system --- without permission in writing from the publisher, except by a reviewer, who may quote brief passages in a review. Published by: Seraph Books.

Cover Design: Alyssa M. Curry
Copy Editing: Alyssa M. Curry
Cover Photo: Belovodchenko Anton

ISBN-13: 978-1-941711-02-6

For information regarding special discounts for bulk purchases of this book for educational or gift purposes, as a charitable donation, or to arrange a speaking event with the author, please contact:

www.Brenda-Blackmon.com
twitter@bbluvu20
www.facebook.com/brenda.blackmon.14

Dedication

To Victims of Domestic Violence

I understand the shame and pain of accepting the fact that you have the labels above. A label is simply a description of something that was given for a particular reason at one point. Don't allow your negative experiences to brand you. The choice to become healed emotionally and mentally is yours.

One of our gifts in life, regardless of whether or not the experiences are joyous or painful, is that we are quite capable of learning from them. Absorb the lesson that will help you grow stronger and wiser, but leave the pain behind. Seek empowerment, education and the ability to protect yourself against abuse so your future will not allow you to be victimized by domestic violence again.

While my experience with domestic violence was both shameful and painful, I have learned three things. First, domestic violence is not something you accept. When it happens and nothing is done about it, that's acceptance. Secondly, regardless of how much you think you love each other, love is not supposed to be painful or violent, so reevaluate how you are defining love. Lastly, if there is not admittance of being an abuser or a victim, the cycle will continue.

In sharing my story, I am exposing personal experiences while offering my perspectives along with alternative actions that should have been considered or taken. If you are reading this and have experienced domestic violence or know someone that has, please recognize the signs provided in this book and use them as a cautionary measure. Allow my story to help lead you along a new path intended to restore your life to a more peaceful state.

With Love,
Brenda Blackmon

ACKNOWLEDGEMENTS

I must first give thanks to God for helping me gain proper knowledge of my strengths. Although we function daily in our aesthetic lives we become so distracted by our eminent ambitions that we lose sight and question our true purpose. I remember discussing my future with my high school counselor. I was uncertain of where my focus would lie until I attended college. At that point, I began to explore diverse cultures, ways of living and experienced the challenges of being a young adult in an unfamiliar environment.

I attended college in Minnesota. Initially, I enrolled in Augsburg College and then the University of Minnesota. I changed my major from medicine to law and ultimately decided upon journalism. I loved retaining what I learned but I was still searching for my passion. I graduated with both a Journalism and Communication Degree and was drawn to the idea of becoming a journalist or reporter. While I completed a few internships in this field, I deviated from that path and created a successful career in the pharmaceutical industry. It's amazing how we decide to venture off in one direction while God has an entirely different plan or destiny for us.

My sales career gave me an opportunity to live in many states including Minnesota, New Jersey, Illinois, Indiana and Kansas. My experiences were vastly different, but cultivated my strength to keep moving forward regardless of the challenges I encountered.

After my divorce, single parenting, enduring layoffs, and rebuilding my life, there is one thing that remained constant, my faith. My marriage brought challenges that had several unpleasant warning signs. Unfortunately, many of them I disregarded because of love and my innate desire not to fail. I lost some of my passion and focus, while trying to keep myself together for my beautiful daughter. And when I looked at her, I'd never want her to endure what I have. No one should be subjected to abuse.

I've written *Living in the Black* with the intent to help others understand the significance of recognizing the signs of abuse. It's vital not to allow shame to overshadow speaking out and ending the vicious cycle of domestic violence. Perhaps, domestic violence continues to exist because we simply don't understand it. Additionally, we aren't aware of the signs that cultivate it.

Some of the obvious signs of abuse are controlling behavior, insecurities, verbal, mental, sexual and physical abuse. However, keep in mind that there are many indicators such as hiding abuse that has occurred in previous generations in hopes that no one will find out. When the topic of family abuse is avoided, that's a sign that it may be allowed to continue.

I'm amazed at how many of my dear friends over the years, having diverse backgrounds and living all over world, have kept quite about their negative experiences regarding abuse. Some have chosen to divorce and move on. Upon reviewing the statistics of abused women that are killed, permanently disfigured, or injured, they were blessed to have had the opportunity and choice to leave, as many others don't.

Marala Scott is a bestselling and award-winning author of the prolific memoir, *In Our House: Perceptions vs. Reality*, *Surrounded by Inspiration*, *Bad to the Bone* and the soul-shaking novel co-authored with her daughter, Alyssa Curry, *Intuition*. She gave me the advice to write this book from my soul, stating, "In there, is where you'll find the truth." That is what I've shared with you. Please accept it knowing it is shared out of love.

I hope after reading *Living in the Black*, you will want to join the countless others helping men, women and children heal and overcome the violent journey they've endured or keep others from taking that journey.

TIDBITS

Healing is complicated because the images are always vivid. You have the strength to use them in a positive manner. No matter how small, there is a remnant that can be used to rebuild.

Living in the Black

www.seraphbooks.com

INTRODUCTION

I grabbed a light jacket hanging in the closet next to the front door, slipped into a pair of comfortable shoes and left the house at 11:47 that evening. The sky was pitch black and a gnawing feeling of disgust churned heavily inside of me. I drove around the city under the streetlights trying to fathom where and what Cedric could be doing. When he left the house a few hours earlier, he said he'd be right back, but the value of his words had long diminished with his incessant predictable behavior. I knew Cedric well and so did a lot of other people. This wasn't the first time he slipped away, only to disappear for hours.

Our relationship wasn't progressing along a healthy path; instead it was picking up speed and heading towards a precipice. Whenever an argument ensued, Cedric and I would remove our rings and threaten to part ways out of either frustration or explosive bouts of anger. After a while, it became a closing segment of the routine, becoming nothing more than a way to temper the dialogue and cool us down. We had some really great times in our marriage but the fights and harsh words eclipsed the beauty.

The lack of comparable vision and defined roles in our household made me feel as though, the majority of time, we weren't on the same page. If I had one perspective, Cedric was sure to support another to cause that division even when we wanted the same thing. There was the stress of buying our first home, work, and several other factors, which contributed to our extremely dysfunctional and volatile exchange of communication.

At the end of a long day, separating work from my personal relationship wasn't my strong point. After leaving work, I'd manage to load my briefcase with projects that needed attention and take them home, only to spend hours working on my computer analyzing my business for the day or week.

While Cedric had his own repertoire of pressure to obtain the proper licensing and bonding to complete a million dollar construction bid, there was a surprise paternity indictment from his previous relationship. She was suing him for child support. And if that didn't add unnecessary stress to the relationship, the uncertainty about having a baby remained. I couldn't understand why I was apprehensive because my due date was only four months away. The time for uncertainty had long departed.

Working tirelessly to hit financial goals and keep our young marriage healthy wasn't the difficult part. It was that we didn't take time to define our roles and set expectations as husband and wife prior to getting married. God was not the foundation of our marriage. Instead, we jumped in and figured we'd handle things as they came along. I didn't pause to consider that far too much damage had already been done, further amassing our unresolved issues. Time didn't make the relationship better, it made the destruction bigger.

There was unfinished business from previous relationships that desperately needed closure but neither of us made time to leave the past where it belonged and move forward into a healthy future. I was focused on the things I wanted in a relationship and found myself connected to the dangerous part of Cedric's charm. Due to the way he was raised, Cedric proclaimed he understood the institution of marriage and believed in its principles. He was from the south and raised in a church so with a great deal of naivety, I believed him. Cedric's father taught his children to love the Lord and respect the word so for some reason I thought those were sufficient guidelines to keep a marriage true to God. There were stages that I wondered if marriage was truly God's institution.

Cedric was a proud man who wrestled with his manhood as it related to being a provider and the leader of our household. The stress of working and the ambiguity of Cedric's drive and passion to be the provider, I believed he was capable of being, always left the appearance that he only kept one foot in the door. It was the other foot that kept straying away, adding excessive tension on the relationship. The arguments were like most young married couples, but I fought out of love and my desire to hold onto Cedric.

Experience taught me that life comes at you hard. When an opportunity presents itself, embrace it passionately before that fleeting moment vanishes. Adapting to change was essential to me. It didn't matter what I was feeling internally because I tried to keep it there. Since your outward behavior is visible and often moods are detectable, that's what people observe. Cedric chose to react to change instead of embracing it making it difficult for me to determine why he was so resistant to change. It caused me to believe he had an insecurity of some sort but I couldn't pinpoint just one. Meanwhile, I remained passionate about most things I did and worked tirelessly to accomplish my goals, but the one thing I didn't want to fail at, was love. I really didn't know why that was such a priority to me, but it was.

It was a few hours before our typical discussion about plans for the baby, work schedules and things that needed to be fixed at home. I understood Cedric was still stressed about the new project he was trying to secure because he was short with me and became irritated when I brought it up. It was 1993 and Cedric was thirty-three years old. Minority contractors weren't always appropriately recognized in Minnesota, which caused additional concern. They had to fight for attention and faced intense scrutiny by inspectors, often having to underbid to secure a contract. Cedric seemed to carry a lot of secrets or concerns but whichever it was; I knew something made him uneasy. Whenever I'd attempt to question him his standard reply was, "It's hard to be a black man."

I couldn't disagree that he had valid reasons that have historically kept people of color behind the eight ball. My issue was that he lacked the initiative to find solutions to correct those problems and implement the necessary effort to move forward.

Cedric and I were both confidant and strong-willed individuals causing discussions to quickly escalate into screaming and fighting. Initially, those discussions appeared to be healthy and vigorous but at some point, they changed. I generally knew what I wanted and didn't hold back in regards to expressing my opinion. Cedric was from a Pentecostal Christian family that celebrated the gift of expression so he didn't suppress anything either.

As time passed, I grew weary of his disrespectful routine noticing that he was gone at random times without incident. Naturally, I began to question his whereabouts because he wasn't hanging around his usual spots either. Sometimes I'd go look for him, walking into one bar after another. I turned a few heads because I was seven months pregnant and going into some of the establishments, alone at night, wasn't wise. However, I thought since I was a familiar face to a few, I'd be okay.

That night I went out to find him. We didn't have an argument or anything that caused him to leave, he just did. So when I entered the second bar, I didn't waste much time, I walk in and headed over to the bartender.

"Hey Joe, have you seen Cedric?" I'd asked trying to sound calm.

"Naw, not tonight, Baby Girl. He was here last weekend. So, how's the baby?" Joe questioned, changing the topic.

I always tired to control my tone to conceal my trepidation about Cedric. "Baby's growing fast and we think it's a girl," I replied with a wide smile.

After thanking him, I'd leave and venture off to continue my search feeling nauseous while rubbing my hand across my growing belly. My search for Cedric grabbed a few hours of my night going in and out of hotspots we used to visit. On this particular evening, I wasn't angry, I just wanted to find my husband and talk to him. I thought that making an attempt to discover his whereabouts would show him that I cared. I hoped he'd realize that it was bothering me.

It was about one-thirty by the time I pulled into our driveway after an unsuccessful pursuit. I clicked the black button on the opener and watched the two-car aluminum door slowly rise. My eyes widened when I saw his car resting in the garage. After all that looking! I was glad he was home, but now I had to contend with his mood. After parking, I got out of the car and shut the door. As I walked past his black car to get to the side door, I touched the hood only to find it was still warm. I went inside, dropped my keys on the glass table in the foyer, took off my shoes and went upstairs to find him lying comfortably in bed.

Not a word was spoken between us as I reached into my side of the white oak dresser for my pajamas. I went into the bathroom, changed my clothes and returned. I quietly sat on the left side of the bed for a few moments before slipping under the blankets beside him.

Cedric turned his body towards me and pointed at my face snapping angrily, "Where in the hell have you been?"

His anger spilled out with the strong smell of alcohol releasing his words. My stomach was tight and looked like a basketball under the white blanket. Growing more uncomfortable by his tone, I covered my stomach with my hands.

In a soft nervous voice I answered, "I went out looking for you. Where were you? You said you'd be right back and you left at eleven."

Cedric knew how to intimidate me. He casted a chilling stare causing me to look away. To get comfortable and avoid an argument from escalating, I laid on my side with my back to Cedric. It didn't take long before everything faded to black.

It was 2:45 the next morning and I was lying on my back in a cold and uninviting room, staring at a white, textured ceiling after praying. When I turned my head to the right, I had the perfect angle to see a few nurses at a desk, not far from the room. They were leaning in towards one another as if they were whispering. Intermittently, they continued to glance into my room. If they were talking about me, they had a good enough reason.

Several thoughts rampantly raced through my mind and I shook my head trying to rid myself of them, only they wouldn't budge. I reached over, grabbed my black purse and pulled out a little gold compact mirror. The last time I looked in the mirror, it was evident that I'd lost sight of who I was, and I didn't do anything to change. I was ashamed that I couldn't recognize myself. My lips, eyes and the side of my face were painfully swollen. I was embarrassed to look at the stranger I'd become because I didn't recognize this person. I considered myself intelligent, loving, hardworking and successful but this ... this was a scenario I never thought I'd see, let alone, experience. My shaking hands slowly closed the compact. I slipped it back inside my purse and moved it aside. This is what it's like *living in the black.*

I thought the stress Cedric withstood because of his job and having to pay child support, may have pushed him to a breaking point. I continually sought an excuse for him to make it more palatable for myself.

I couldn't help but reminiscence about the call I received a few years prior to marrying Cedric. It was from his ex-girlfriend. The woman was hesitant yet ardent in her attempt to warn me about Cedric. I assumed she was upset or jealous about our relationship and quickly dismissed her claims, ending the conversation rather brashly. But after the first forceful strike Cedric rendered to my face, I swiftly recanted her fervent words of warning and put it together. She was trying to forewarn me about Cedric's violent outrage but *I refused to listen.* I wasn't ready to hear anything from another woman, especially his ex. I assumed that she was scorned and miserable so she wanted to make sure Cedric was too. I wasn't willing to give her the opportunity to vent about what was wrong in their relationship because it had nothing to do with me. I wouldn't know if she were lying or not so I ended the call. Besides, I didn't think I could handle one more thing regarding his history. When you love someone being happy shouldn't be difficult and I didn't want to search for reasons not to be.

When Cedric wasn't working at his construction company, he kept the house in pretty good order. And when he cooked, I swear that man would leave me begging for more. It was easy for me to focus on the good things he did. Cedric and I planned on enjoying our life together and we weren't afraid to work hard to have a good one. We'd often envision things that would make our life together beautiful. Sadly, everything faded into obscurity and my mind quickly snapped back from my dreams to what put me in the hospital bed.

Already trying to forget the traumatic ordeal and gather what little self-esteem I had, I wondered how long it would take for my black eyes to heal before I could return to work. I needed to focus on something other than where I was and what I'd undoubtedly end up going back to. Work was something I did well. I loved working because it offered a constant reprieve from my reality. I'd seen glimpses of this but would often shrug it off thinking his mood would end.

I was pondering how to explain this to my boss because it was unlikely that I could conceal my face or hide the obvious abuse from my colleagues. I valued my position in the pharmaceutical industry and being a positive resource for the Minneapolis community was important to me. I was an advocate for a women's organization for abuse victims, which was a local rescue program that provided food, cell phones, clothing and more to women that fled from an abusive relationship to start a new life on their own. I was well versed on the staggering amount of women worldwide that suffer from physical, mental, and emotional abuse from a spouse or significant other. I'd become a part of those statistics.

The doctor returned to my room and carefully began examining me. He gently touched specific areas of my belly causing me to inhale quickly. All I could do was grit my teeth and withdraw from his touch. The doctor asked me a series of questions while he continued checking my facial bones and head before closely taking a look at the scratches around my eyes. Finally, he said, "Luckily, it appears that nothing's broken. The swelling and bruises should disappear in a few weeks."

Upon my arrival to the emergency room, the health care providers ran a few tests and determined that the baby was unharmed. I couldn't shake off the feeling I was overcome with because I never imagined being in that position. The thought of being a battered woman made me feel sick. I was angry and disgusted by this outcome because Cedric and I planned on having a perfect marriage. The love we had for one another was supposed to last forever. What was this? Where did it come from? And how did it turn to this so fast? I acted as if I didn't know.

I laid my head back on the pillow and allowed everything from that morning to replay in my head like the scenes from a traumatizing movie. The receptionist checked me into the hospital after asking a series of questions. Clearly in her routine of having done this numerous times, without looking up, she asked my name and address. Rapidly tapping away at the keyboard, she continued to request my personal information without leaving much time for a reply.

"Do you have insurance? If so, I need to make a copy of it to put on file," she continued.

I reached inside my purse, retrieved the little white insurance card from my wallet and slid it across the desk, next to her keyboard. She popped up from her desk and casually walked over to the copier. When she returned and handed me my card, her green eyes met mine for the first time, but my face was concealed with a scarf. Her eyebrows arched together and a rather inquisitive expression flashed across her face.

"And … what's the nature of your visit?" she asked curiously before she sat down.

Without breaking eye contact, I removed the scarf and revealed my face, "I need to be examined to make sure that my baby and I are okay. I'm … seven months pregnant."

This time, her face displayed an unspoken look of compassion for my pain. She sat down gently in her black chair, exhaled slowly and returned to her typing. The receptionist stole a glance at Cedric sitting beside me and sluggishly shook her head, but he quickly turned away. Fuming, she returned her eyes back to the computer screen and continued to type, tapping harder on the keyboard than she had before as I answered the rest of her questions.

With more sympathy in her voice, the receptionist said, "Someone will be here to speak with you after the doctor have done a full check-up." Each word slowly rolled off her tongue and sounded like an echo, but I understood what she meant. The police would be asking if I wanted to press charges. I could feel Cedric's gaze, but I ignored him for the time being. I had not yet accepted that my husband abused me! More than anything, I was in pain, not just from the marks and swelling, but from embarrassment. I quickly understood why some women hid the shame, but I needed to be there, if not for anything else, for our baby. After the receptionist was finished, I read and signed the patient-doctor confidentiality agreement and waiting quietly to be taken back.

I had attended training seminars for Women Taking Risks and learned that abusive husbands claim they will change; promising not to do it again. There are men that appear charming and passionate, but it's a mask to conceal their true personality. I always thought I knew better but now I was in that situation. I was afraid because I didn't know how things would play out.

As I slowly recovered emotionally, my quest was focused on forgiving and gaining the strength to share my story with others within the organizations I was familiar with. I wanted to encourage and inspire women to take action. But at that very moment, the idea of pressing charges against my husband seemed foreign to me. How could I allow my mind to drift over to thinking about legal action? I was trying to wrap my mind around what happened to me but I was at a complete loss. I visualized the other incidents that led Cedric's hands in places I didn't imagine they'd ever go with force he used. The person I married wasn't who I thought he was. I respect love. I believed you were commitment to that person, communicated with them properly, and were dedicated to protecting them. A husband was supposed to love his wife but Cedric was no longer doing that.

Although I hadn't told anyone, that wasn't the first time. On another occasion, Cedric restrained me by straddling my legs so I couldn't move. He began to break me with such ease and I could tell he enjoyed it. Whatever was hurting him, he was taking out on me. Both of my hands were pinned beneath one of his massive hands so I couldn't block the blows he rendered to my face. Cedric first landed a strike with an open hand to the right side of my face and then a backhand to the other side. I could taste blood coming from the inside of my cheeks due to the force from them slamming into my teeth. I tried to plead with him by saying, "I'm sorry, I didn't mean to do it! What about the baby?" However, none of that mattered. He continued as I begged for his forgiveness. I didn't do it to apologize or because I needed to, but his blows made me believe that if I submitted to him, the ordeal would cease. It never stopped until he was ready, which further empowered him.

It took a while but I realized that Cedric had a different agenda. His method was to control and destroy. In the moment of each strike, which felt painful and then numbing, I remembered thinking that this was the beginning of my demise. I continued to plead, but he only hit harder until I felt my mind and body losing consciousness before everything faded to black.

My return to full consciousness was a struggle. The cool air drifted across my taut body giving me a slight chill. I was lying on the floor looking up at the white ceiling slowly trying to rotate my aching head to the right. I caught a glimpse of Cedric out of my one good eye and watched him crying with his head resting in his heavy hands. In a low repetitive mumble he said, "It's okay, it'll be alright. God, it's not supposed to be like this." I released a slight cough and he removed his hands and saw my eye blink. His expression let me know he was happy that I was conscious. I didn't know how long I'd been lying there and I alleged it didn't matter because he hadn't done anything about it. He delivered his words more fervently now that I was conscious or alive.

"Baby please, can we get some ice? It'll be okay if we put some ice on it. Everything will be okay," he advised, sounding as if the reality of what he'd done was seeping in.

Sensitive to every painful movement, I grabbed onto the edge of the dresser and pulled myself to a sitting position. I sat there for a few moments trying to gather my senses and composure but I felt dizzy when I stood up. Without saying a word, I stumbled my way into the bathroom. I flicked the light switch on, moved over to the sink and held onto the countertop to keep my balance. Assessing the damage, I was looking at someone I didn't recognize. Horrified and in disbelief to the reflection of a badly battered woman with busted lips, swelling around the left eye and bruises on the ballooned cheeks. I opened the door and returned to the bedroom to face him and cried out, "The baby! We have to go to the hospital. Look at my face. Look at me!" The thought something could be wrong with our baby rendered me panic-stricken. I didn't know how long I'd been on the floor but he seemed to think that *ice* would make everything better. He didn't display any concern for our child growing inside of me.

My elation over the baby was beginning to dissipate because I was fearful of his ability to snap into such an abusive episode, his competency, and ability to be a good father became a frightening concern. The last thing I wanted to become was a single mom with a child living in a broken family.

While lying in the hospital bed, I recalled a recent story in the news where witnesses reported seeing a man choking a woman in the parking lot of a restaurant. The police arrested him but he was released because the woman refused to press charges. Two weeks later, the same couple was back in the news, but this time, he had killed her.

I understood some statistics of abuse might be lower than the true number because the data only includes those who report it. People really don't want to hear the continuum of abusive occurrences when many believe you should just make the decision to stop it and leave. When a man beats his wife, degrades or controls her, most people blame the woman as if she deserved it. Generally, there's someone that's aware of what's occurring but they refuse to truly acknowledge it or speak up. If you don't, why should they? So they don't. And they stay out of it leaving the victim to wonder why no one will help. At times, we have to help ourselves first before others will believe we want it.

Abuse tends to have a pattern of controlling mechanisms. This could be physical force, verbal, mental distress, sexually or beatings and fear is their goal. There is always a pattern that develops and signs that are indicators. I disregarded the ones presented to me and didn't comprehend the small insignificant incidents that occurred early in my relationship would manifest into an abusive pattern. The fear of having a failed marriage was the motivating factor that caused me to stay committed.

There are a tremendous amount of misconceptions about physical abuse, victims and abusers. Victims are thought of as weak or vulnerable because they stay and allow the abuse to continue. Often, abuse becomes a secret that's kept from friends and family members, out of shame. Sometimes people may have an idea of what's occurring and want to help yet, they don't know how or in what capacity. I never shared my unfortunate circumstances with my mom, sister or brother although; they were knowledgeable that Cedric and I argued frequently. No one asked anything further. I believed that they thought that since I stayed with him, we'd worked things out between us and that it was my business, husband and life. Knowing how I valued my privacy, they were right because that was the impression I presented.

I recall discussing the issue with my brother-in-law, whom was a pastor. I told him I needed to be divorced and move on with my life. However, I was bewildered at the fact that he implored me to reconsider the divorce and recommended that *I*, not we, make the marriage work.

CHAPTER 1
MY HISTORY

My family and I lived in a two-story building on the corner of Erie and 10th Street. My Mom was born in Chicago and had roots in Georgia while my Dad was born in Mississippi. He moved to Chicago in the '50s after spending time in the Air Force. When I was twelve years old, my father lost his battle to cancer and passed away, leaving me with a tremendous void. My parents rarely talked about their parents, so as far as I knew, my family tree ceased there.

I grew up on the West Side of Chicago. As a child, I was given a loose leash and provided the opportunity to explore the neighborhood and people around me. As a young teen, I sat on the front porch and watched people in the neighborhood. I knew everyone, from the corner drunk to the respectable judge who lived ten miles away in a massive home. The neighborhood I grew up in was a great melting pot. It was a middle class neighborhood with a sprinkle of lower income families blended in. The upper West Side of Chicago was an old community with a mixture of large and small brick, two-flat buildings. Most of them had medium-sized lots with a front and back yard. The community as a whole was vintage because of the authentic exterior décor styles and the original infrastructure that remained after many years. Back in the late '70s, the city of Chicago wanted to build a strip mall in the area. This would have caused the center of the Upper West Side to be demolished or replaced with office buildings and parking lots. The community residents consisted of the men and women that were involved in the Civil Rights Movement in the '60s. Those who organized, campaigned, and worked behind the scenes to support those who spoke out against racial inequalities and injustices. My father, Cole, spoke out against the impending development and rallied the neighborhood homeowners to petition against it. He convinced twenty-five hundred owners and residents of the Upper West Side community to sign a petition that blocked the demolition of forty-five homes, townhomes and apartment buildings.

My father was viewed as a hero to the neighborhood and he had continued to work beyond what was expected. One night, several teenagers broke into an elderly woman's home. They terrorized the woman, stole her possessions and trashed her home. The police had arrested the wrong suspects for the break-in so my father raised bail money for the kids. The case was later dismissed due to a lack of sufficient evidence. My father had done his own investigation within the neighborhood to find the people responsible and eventually convinced the offenders to confess to the crime. Bullies feed off of others' fear, but deep down inside, they're cowardly and vulnerable.

My father, Cole, was a large man with a serious demeanor and a voice to be reckoned with. He opposed violence. Dad was firm and direct when it came to demanding respect and expecting others to align themselves with the right actions. He was a blueprint advocating for a safe community uninhibited by undesirable characters. Not only was he involved in the community, but he provided for his family as well.

Cole and Patti were high school sweethearts and my mother, Patti, was right by his side ever since. I loved my parents and they were a perfect couple in my eyes. My strength came from watching them interact as husband and wife. I grew up in the '60s and '70s where marriage was honorable back then. Men seemed to cherish their partner while women were more submissive and honored their companion. My parents married when they were pregnant with my older sister, but they struggled like any young couple in the '60s.

Regardless of everything, what kept our family bonded together was the love and respect we had for each other. I watched Dad work every day to provide for his family. In addition, he became a voice that the community recognized as a leader. He wasn't perfect, but he worked diligently to sustain being the protector that a man should be for his family. Mom fell in love with him from the moment they met and was only nineteen when they married. I watched my mother serve Dad his meals and keep things in around the house in order. Meanwhile, she worked part-time at the post office and eventually went back to college to get her degree. However, home was not without its struggles or setbacks. It was unity and respect that allowed my parents to work through their differences, which allowed them to reach for the zest of life. Some things were put on the back burner after my sister and I came into the picture.

As a young girl, I was the most energetic child and enjoyed playing outside. Riding bikes and playing basketball were my favorite outdoor activities. I had a blue bike with a light blue and white banana seat. Six-inch white fringes hung from each handle and one was tied to the banana seat.

When I was nine years old, a young boy chased me on foot while I rode my bike. I gripped the long handlebars tightly and my legs moved at lighting speed, but the boy's hand reached the tip of my blue banana seat. His grip on the seat caused me to lose my balance. When I released my feet from the pedals, they began to skid across the concrete until I lost total control. The bike crashed, causing my left shoulder and elbow to scrape across the cement. While I was in the process of regaining my composure, the young boy eagerly tried to pick up the bike and peal off. Before he could, I gripped his leg tightly and pulled him back to the ground. I was able to push myself up to a standing position. When he stood up, we both balled up our fists and began swinging at one another while my bike fell to the ground again. I continuously kicked and threw punches with an uncalculated ferociousness until the boy finally backed off and ran away. My clothes and hair were all out of place. When I looked down, I noticed that my elbow and knees were bleeding. After a moment of standing there in disbelief, trying to gather my composure, I smoothed the hair off my face into a messy ponytail. Still seething, I grabbed the handlebars and headed home. The oily, black residue from the chain left small marks on the pavement at the scene of the incident and the chain dragged for two miles until I could see our brick, two-flat building.

Someone in the neighborhood must have seen what happened because word spread and no one attempted to bother me again. I was a small, petite kid, but determination and "fight or flight" gave me the strength to fight when it was necessary. Being strong-willed and protective of the things that belonged to me was an integral part of my character, which became my forte.

    My first love was sports. I had the ability to learn by watching and imitating others. I would always watch the older girls complete full court suicides, half court dribbling drills and play scrimmage games. As I watched the hand movements and how the basketball had a magnetic connection to their hands, even while sprinting down the court, I knew that I wanted to play. I was good at shooting the ball and wasn't a bad ball handler, but didn't consider playing organized basketball. When I did play, it was typically in the alley with the neighborhood kids. When I first tried out for the A team, I was the only fifth grader.

    The basketball court was slick, but I concentrated on keeping the basketball below the waist. The coach yelled, "Don't lose control of the ball, balance, look straight head, and don't lose control!" My tennis shoes didn't really have enough of a grip because they were old, tattered and weren't exclusively used for basketball practice. In the back of my mind, I was thinking about how to ask my dad for a pair of the brand new, white Chuck Taylor's. I wasn't the best at maneuvering the ball, but compared to the other girls at practice, my skills were somewhat impressive. That didn't matter too much because I knew I would have the dedication to progress. There were two teams at St. Paul Elementary school, Team A for sixth through eighth grade and Team B for fifth grade. After the first hour, the head coach and the coaching assistant pulled me aside and gave me extra attention because they could sense the skill and promise in what I brought to the court. I made the A team and played guard with all my heart. I fell in love with the game. It was truly due to hard work and practice. I was a believer that if I focused, studied and practiced, I could learn just about anything. No only did I apply that to basketball, but to school, as well.

I went to a small Lutheran school affiliated with the American Lutheran Church. At school, there was always a team effort to teach, counsel and prepare kids in all grades to be ready for high school. As I transformed from a preadolescent to a teenager in seventh grade, I admired and respected one of my substitute teachers. She was a thin, quite woman with a big smile and a demeanor like Condoleezza. She was in her early '30s, had small features and lines formed around her mouth whenever she smiled. Ms. Decker substituted in the afternoons during social studies and literature in lieu of the principal. At the time, I didn't understand why she mesmerized me nor did I understand that having a crush on a female teacher was a heinous crime. Kids talk and it was clear that many of the students, girls and boys, had a crush on Ms. Decker, too. My parents never talked about sexual relations, homosexuality or same sex relationships back in the '70s. As a young teenager, I knew what was right and what was wrong, but that didn't stop me from thinking about Ms. Decker during lunch break and I looked forward to attending class on the days when she substituted. During homework, I thought about her smile and I could almost smell her perfume in my room. I made sure that I was dressed in my best school clothes on the days that Ms. Decker taught. Ms. Decker wore square, black glasses and I would flash a smile every time she pushed her glasses up the ridge of her nose. I enjoyed watching her because it seemed that every time she did the quirky little move, Ms. Decker appeared to be looking at me, even if she wasn't. During a class field trip, she said, "Hi Brenda, you look pretty today. How's it going with you?" I walked along side of her as the rest of the class followed behind. She was dressed in a new red and white sundress with ruffled short sleeves and white tennis shoes. During a conversation, Ms. Decker told me that she began her teaching career in North Chicago, IL and enjoyed substituting for Mr. Roush. Eventually other kids joined in, asking Ms. Decker more questions about herself and the sights of the museum we were touring. I saved my event ticket, graded homework papers with Ms. Decker's comments on them and the hall passes with her signature tucked away in my souvenir box.

When Ms. Decker was on staff at school, it seemed like there were more field trips and excitement in the classroom. During one of her lessons, she said "History is important because it always repeats itself. It is a collaboration of everything that will happen to us. We look at the past and predict the future." I could see the passion in her eyes as she'd ask the class to imagine what the United States would be like if the Spanish found it before we did. "Because Americans found the land that is now America, we can look back at that event and analyze our forefathers' efforts and continue down the path they created." She would venture deep into conversations about family and genealogy. Once, Ms. Decker asked everyone to pair up with someone new to learn about his or her family history. The class had to interview their partner, discover something that connected each other and then write a report about their uniqueness and the emotions it caused. The next day, each student presented what he or she learned to the class. On this particular day, a few students were absent which made the total number of students uneven and Ms. Decker paired up with me. During this class exercise, I became even more infatuated.

I learned that Ms. Decker was originally from Cameroon and that she grew up on a farm. When she and her family moved to the United States, everyone pitched in and worked to provide for the family. As a young girl, she was tutored in English by a neighbor and a few years after, became a tutor for others who immigrated into her neighborhood. She was passionate about giving back to the community. She told me that when she was a little girl in Cameroon, her mother and grandmother made sure that young girls in her community had school supplies, food and personal items no matter what social economic class they lived in. Her mother and grandmother were social ambassadors for the village education of all girls. Before marriage, the young woman is equipped with an education, cooking and financial skills so that she could contribute to the success of their growing family. The female education ambassadors ensured that this tradition withstood through decades. Ms. Decker appreciated those who needed to be uplifted and feel that they were a part of something. She learned the proper English language and shared her knowledge freely. Her native French dialect never faded, but her English and literary skills became one to be desired and eventually led to her becoming the Director of Education. She received her PhD. in Education from Cornell University in New York City. During my interview with her, I discovered that Ms. Decker's grandfather and my grandfather both shared crops on the same farm back in Mississippi.

The whole experience impacted me in many ways. I learned to communicate with someone on a much higher level than typical without being intimidated. Most students back in the '70s were good kids and respected authority. At times, a few would rebel, but in a way where they could develop and learn to be independent.

Most parents lived up to their responsibility as role models so there was respect, even in the poorest of neighborhoods. I was in the middle. Although I wanted attention, I didn't want to be the center of attention. I wanted everyone to like me so I didn't show an interest in choosing sides nor was I confrontational. However, I would fight if provoked or felt I had to defend myself. My preference was to talk my way out of any fragile situation. I was normally quite and well behaved around Ms. Decker. At least that was the case until I met Ms. Decker's younger brother. That was one of those situations when I dared to be rebellious. I learned how complicated love could be. My heart pounded in my chest when I heard his voice, but I cried when I was forbidden to hear it again.

Ms. Decker taught me to be spontaneous and to act on what I felt. I discovered love was a force inside of me that could cause me to do things I wouldn't normally do. Giving love came easy when Devon's charm and attention showered me. It felt natural for me to respond to someone who persistently demonstrated feelings for me. Although I was self-conscious about what people would think, it didn't suppress my love for Devon. It wasn't that I didn't know how to love, but I didn't know the way to express it outside of the love I showed for my family. I admired my family and wanted to be smart, intelligent, feminine, successful and beautiful. However, I thought I would never be like them, which began my struggle for loving myself.

Ultimately, I learned that when an individual is comfortable in his or her own skin, loving someone else comes naturally. I wasn't the overly feminine, girly type but I did have a desire to be appealing. Ultimately, I had more sensitive characteristics and gentle qualities that gradually took form. I took this as an opportunity to become comfortable with whom I was. Additionally, I was beginning to love who I was. Since I was still a virgin and had not experienced a sexual or emotional connection with anyone, I didn't grasp that there was a difference between being in love and being sexually attracted to a boy. However, I quickly learned the difference after meeting, Devon.

My parents showed love and affection for one another, but oddly, I never heard them say, "I love you." It seemed premeditated when they were around Teri, Christian and I. It wasn't until I became an adult with my own family did I say those words to my family, husband and daughter. As I listened to my young daughter, I realized the strong affect parents have on their children whether or not they realize it.

My daughter tells her family and friends she loves them, but it genuinely comes from the heart. My daughter didn't question her value because she loves herself unconditionally, which is a trait I didn't possess at that age. I used to wonder if my upbringing and environment taught me to mask my feelings or if I was hiding what I didn't like about myself. Although it took time to find a resolve, I was able to recognize that Devon helped me. Devon was my secret fantasy come true.

It was September in 1976. I went shopping with my big sister on a picturesque Sunday afternoon. Teri was only a year older, but I felt safe with her because she knew downtown like it was her regular hang out. I was sixteen-years-old and invited to a Teachers Gala sponsored by the NACCP. Ms. Decker invited two other students as well as Devon. Ms. Decker's mission was to help promote positive images of African Americans. She enjoyed providing the opportunity for teenagers to see what was going on in the world and become involved in the community.

Teri and I headed to my favorite department store Marshalls, because the clothes were stylish and inexpensive. We took the 'L' Train from the West side to downtown Chicago, which was called the Loop. The city's blueprint shows seventy-seven community areas that loop into the center of the city. The Loop was the center of all the action, which included the abundance of shops, restaurants and theatre.

We exited the southbound 'L' Train and ran down the stairs onto the sunlit sidewalk. When we walked into Marshalls, we could see the first floor was full of new fall blazers, dresses, sweaters, jeans and jackets. I didn't waste time heading for the dress rack while Teri ventured off to look at jeans. After wandering through the store, I found myself stationary in front of a slender mannequin. It was modeling a jet-black maxi dress with a faux wrap at the waist. It wasn't the dress that caught my attention; it was the pair of deep red, two-inch, patent leather stacks. They were just high enough to make any teenager feel striking. The stacks were lined with a white stripe on the top of the wedge heel and on each heel were two small, white butterflies. The top of the shoes had a thick white leather strap that tied around the angle in a bow. I was a shoe fanatic and loved to match my outfits with my shoes because I felt they were the most important part of a wardrobe. I found a sales associate and asked if that brand of shoe was for sale or if it was only a display shoe. The woman told me that they were on sale in the shoe department downstairs. First, I went looking for Teri and when I didn't see her I was certain she'd be in the dressing room trying on a pair of blue jeans. I called into the dressing room, "Teri, I want you to see these shoes. They're perfect for the dinner on Saturday."

"Did you find a dress already?" she asked.

"No, but you have to see these shoes. I want to try them on," I replied eagerly.

Teri laughed and said, "You always do things backwards. How do you know if they'll match your dress if you don't have one picked out yet?" She was right. I hadn't thought about it. All I knew was that I loved those shoes. Teri opened the dressing room door with a pair of washed blue Vanderbilt jeans and a white, long sleeve pullover draped across her left arm and told the sales assistant, "I'll take these." She handed the Calvin Klein's to the sales assistant who put them on the return rack. Teri motioned her right hand for me to go forward and take her to the shoes I was ranting about.

We walked toward the escalator, got on and took it down to the shoe department. The apparel and shoes took up the entire lower level. Belts, hats, stockings, purses, braided hobo handbags, shoes and more. Filled with complete excitement, I led Teri to the Lipstick Allí display. The sign read *'Walk if you dare.'* There was a picture of a young teenager walking down a dark alley with confidence and she was smiling. She was wearing the black and dark red wrap dress the mannequin had on upstairs. The imagery presented the perception that she was headed to the most exciting event you could imagine. The look she had in her eyes made me feel like a million dollars after previously feeling uncertain of going to the NAACP dinner. For some reason, I always felt as though I needed to impress my favorite teacher so I dug into my purse and didn't hesitate to spend everything I had. The maxi dress and shoes belonged to me. Teri had some cash remaining from her purchase and used it to buy me a pair of stockings that went well with the dress and shoes. Now I felt I was ready for the NAACP event that following Saturday.

I felt as if our mission was accomplished. I found the perfect dress and shoes to wear while Teri left with a casual outfit for herself. It was nearly 7:00 that evening when we gathered our shopping bags and headed back to the station. The normal Sunday evening crowd had not developed yet. As we walked up the 'L' Station stairs to enter the North bound platform, we could see a crowd exiting the South bound train on the opposite side of the tracks. The crowds' feet were shuffling in unison down the adjacent stairs. I could overhear conversations about the Sunday night movies at the State Theatre. *The Eye of the Tiger*, *Sinbad*, *Close Encounters of the Third Kind*, and *Saturday Night Live* were all competitors.

Teri and I put coins in the slot box and walked through the metal, turn-style entrance. About two hundred yards from the platform entrance were unoccupied, hard wooden benches. We walked over, sat down and rested our shopping bags on our laps. Teri smiled and said, "You did a good job picking out your dress and shoes. Lipstick Allí is one of the new up-and-coming clothing and shoe lines for teens. You'll get some attention when you walk through that ballroom door." She nudged my right shoulder with her elbow emitting a fleeting look from the corner of her eye. Teri had a radiant, brown complexion, large, dark caramel eyes with a perfectly proportionate nose. She had a shapely figure even though she was slender. Nearly everything she wore had to be pressed and in style. I looked up to Teri and I could see that she was truly proud of me for growing into a young lady. I couldn't help but to lean my head back and look at her with a big smile assuring my sister that she was right. I heard the screeching sound of the breaks before the train reached the platform. When it finally came to a stop and the glass doors slid open, people rushed out the door and down the stairs. We quickly slipped inside and found seats towards the back of the car.

I noticed an attractive guy with a smooth cocoa skin tone sporting a short curly afro enter the same car and sit a few seats in front of us. He dropped a few shopping bags from Marshalls at his feet. I briefly wondered why we didn't see him before realizing the men's department was on a different floor. The aroma of his Old Spice cologne gently reached my nose, reminding me of our father's traditional scent. I considered Old Spice to have a faint smell that exuded cleanliness and good hygiene. He turned and shyly stole a glance at me, but I promptly diverted my attention out the window. I felt embarrassed that I'd been caught staring.

Everything appeared to be moving at the speed of light to the point where it morphed into nothing but grey. I could easily discern the variances between environments based on the people. The way they walked, dressed and notable hygiene was often an indication of the type of area we were passing through. When the train stopped at Lombard Street I'd observe the well-manicured grass surrounding the homes situated in the slight distance from the train station. When the train stopped closer to where we lived, near Central and Cicero Avenue, there was brown dirt or cement where once standing buildings had been demolished. The ghetto was an understatement when describing this area. Everyone on the train seemed to tightly grip their purses, brief cases, shopping bags and other belongings as people boarded. My thoughts quickly shifted to next Saturday.

Ms. Decker said she wanted me to meet her little brother, Devon. I considered it an honor because I was one of her special students. I thought it meant

Devon would be escorting me to the event. A special invitation from the best teacher at my school was held in the highest esteem. I must have good timing because the outfit I just purchased was guaranteed to turn heads, at least from the perspective of a sixteen year old. I wasn't one to get dressed up and look girly. I liked wearing dresses to church and for special occasions, but never really dressed up with the intention of pleasing a boy. There was a lot of talk about Devon prior to meeting him, but I felt I had to look a certain way when I attended the ceremony. I didn't want to disappoint Ms. Decker. I felt Ms. Decker spoke about me to Devon in the same manner she told me about him. The impression she left was that Devon liked young women who could speak their mind and look sweet, but still have an interest in sports. The anticipation was so intense; I believed I was giving too much focus on how I should look. Somehow, I thought that it was the attention that I needed.

Our stop was fifteen minutes away. When I looked over at Teri, she seemed relaxed. Once the train picked up its pace again, it was easy to lay back and take a nap because one could instinctively tell when someone was supposed to get off the train. It didn't take much for Teri to doze off when she wanted to.

My shopping bags rested on the train floor in between my feet. I was intrigued by the shoebox and wanted to take a look again. I lifted the bag onto my lap and opened the drawstrings just enough to see the red and gold Lipstick Allí emblem. The emblem was similar to an official raised seal, but instead of an eagle being imprinted, there was a tilted red high heel shoe with the perfect set of red lips in the inset. The impression on an emblem was supposed to represent the original version of the item. Looking at the box itself, it was not the normal corrugated cardboard. It looked like it was painted with an expensive glossy paint. I ran my fingers along the side of the box knowing it would be a keepsake. I returned the box to the bag and pushed it back down on the floor, between my feet. I thought about the excitement of possibly being the first person at school to wear this shoe line.

The train rolled to a stop, the fiberglass and steel doors flew open for more people to get on and off. Oak Street was the urban affluent area. Mansions with huge manicured yards, refurbished brownstones, upscale retail stores and perfectly paved sidewalks surrounded it. The new passengers settled in to the partially crowded train car and the train accelerated once again. I always felt comfortable knowing that someone with me would stay alert if I fell asleep on the train but this time Teri slept while I was thinking about Devon.

I couldn't get my mind off the fact that Ms. Decker was so intent on me meeting Devon. The only time I ever kissed a boy was at my sixteenth birthday party. Junior was one of the neighborhood kids who played softball with our recreation center team. He was short, athletic and the best softball pitcher in the recreation league.

When he rang the doorbell and entered the living room with the most decorative birthday box in hand that past December, I barely recognized him because he looked so handsome. At the party, Junior was the person who stuck by me and helped with things like replenishing the snack dishes and bringing out the cake. When all the kids started dancing, he was there with his hand out, ready to escort me to the living room floor to dance. Junior and I danced to an Isley Brothers slow song that was playing. I wrapped my arms around his broad shoulders while he positioned his hands around my waist. We were about six inches from each other when I recalled two main rules my mom had when it came to boys. No boys in the house unless she authorized it and no slow dancing or grinding. Since my mom allowed the lights to be off, except a small light coming from the corner near the food, I knew she would allow me to have that moment to slow dance. As Ronald Isley's beautiful falsetto voice sang, "Driftin' on a memory ain't no place I'd rather be then with you ..." Junior pulled me closer and placed a wild kiss on my month while slipping his tongue in. I closed my eyes and returned the kiss enthusiastically. Once I figured out that there was a rhythm to kissing, our movement became in sync and grew stronger. Most of my friends had already explored further with a guy, but my kiss with Junior had been my first experience in that area.

    I snapped out of reminiscing when I heard the screeching of the breaks once again. The attendant announced Cicero as the next stop and told us to prepare to exit. Teri sat up and said, "This is our stop; make sure you don't forget your bags." I gathered my shopping bags and exited the train. Teri and I walked eight blocks from the train station to our house. During the walk, Teri shared how proud she was of me for being independent and finding my own style. She advised me to be on my best behavior and polite while I was at the event. Although Teri was only a year older than me, she made it a priority to lead me in the right direction and look after me. I couldn't imagine not having Teri in my life because she was like a mentor. She was my rock.

When Teri rang the doorbell, mom answered and excitedly exclaimed, "There are my favorite girls! How'd it go at Marshalls?"

As I nudged Teri with my elbow, I said, "We did good and had a lot of fun. I'll show you." I gave Mom a hug and hurried to my room to try everything on. After shopping, I always enjoyed showing my parents because to me it was a sign of independence. As well, Teri and I made sure mom lived vicariously through us by giving her every detail of our adventures. I tried on my new dress with the matching control top stockings and wedge-heel shoes. I strutted down the kitchen hallway, from one end to the other with poise and determination. Slowly, I turned halfway to the right and then to the left with sassiness and confidence. Then I stood up straight and held my head back as I spun around. I could see the wide smiles on their face as the dizziness wore off. I gave them the best fashion show I could. Showing off made me feel confident about my shopping choices and excitement about the event amplified.

"Brenda, you look stunning! You're all grown up," Mom shouted.

My stepdad interjected, "You look beautiful, but watch out for those boys," he added, allowing a light-hearted laugh to escape.

Later, Mom was finishing the final touches on her pork chops, mash potatoes and gravy for dinner. Meanwhile, Teri and I were assembling a salad. All of us had specific things we were responsible for around the house. My brother, Christian, set the table and Dad blessed the meal. After we enjoying dinner as a family, Teri put Palm Olive dish soap in the sink with hot water and agigated it to make lots of suds. She scraped the food off the plates and soaked them in water before washing them. Once the dishes were washed, I dried each one and put it in its place. Christian swept the floors and wiped down the countertops. I liked that we worked as a unit.

After we finished cleaning the kitchen, I did some homework and got ready for bed. Teri and I shared a bedroom in the back of the house near the kitchen. If the rest of the family gathered in the kitchen for conversation, Teri and I could hear every word. Christian had the bedroom near the front door.

The week went by fast. I had a standard routine of school, along with basketball and band practice afterwards. On Friday nights, Mom washed my hair in the kitchen sink. I hated getting my hair done because it was so thick and when it was washed, it expanded and puffed up like a brillo pad. It took at least an hour and a half just to comb out the wet kinks and detangle my hair. Mom would take a handful at a time and comb it from the ends to the roots of my hair. Once a section was untangled, she'd braid it and start on another section. I was tender headed so my scalp was sore after being washed and braided. However, nothing hurt worse than getting my hair pressed. After my hair air-dried, Mom would open a jar of pressing oil while letting the steel iron pressing comb heat up on the left burner of the stove. She'd turn off the burner, let it cool a bit, then grabbed the comb by its calphalon coated handle and get started. She'd put a dab of the pressing oil on one of the unbraided braids and comb through the section. When Mom finished my hair, it was thick, and dropped straight down to my shoulders. Mom curled my hair by adding 3-inch hard, plastic rollers and then she'd tie my hair up in a silk scarf until the next day.

On Saturday morning, I got up at about 10:00 and took a bath. The steam in the bathroom moistened my hair and left a wavy texture around the plastic rollers. When I removed the rollers, the curls fell slowly and bounced freely. I didn't want the curls to be too tight so I'd let them hang free most of the day. It was 4:00 in the evening when I began to excitedly get dressed for the NAACP event. The day felt like it crept so slowly, but finally it was time.

Teri drove me to the Marriott Hotel in downtown Chicago. I got out of the car eagerly shutting the door. Immediately, the crowd and the look of the hotel took me by surprise. This was my first event independent of anyone else. Interrupting my grand thoughts was Teri yelling from the car to get my attention, "Hey!" I quickly spun around to see a bright smile spread across her beautiful face. "Get inside and enjoy yourself. Be bold and confident!" I nodded without delay, turn back around and proceeded through the revolving glass doors. The first thing I noticed was the NAACP Who's Who Awards Ceremony listed at the top of the event board. The announcement was printed in an Aharoni font with a red velvet background and neatly placed in a glass frame. President's Ballroom was listed next to it. The bottom of my dress had a slight loose flair that gently rose up as I walked. When I approached the concierge desk, I politely asked the gentleman sitting behind the mahogany activity desk where the President's Ballroom was located. He directed me to go down the stairs and around to the left until I saw the double doors with an eagle plaque on them. As I walked toward the door the voices grew louder and there was instrumental music playing in the background. I opened the door and scanned the crowd of widely diverse people. There were at least 300 people in the ballroom corridor.

My wrap dress and red patent leather, ankle strap shoes fit in well with all of the other young people in the crowd. My curly hairstyle fell to the tip of my shoulders and stood out while most of the young girls had their hair up. I wasn't much for wearing makeup, but Teri insisted that I wear a little bit of her bat-winged mascara and red lipstick to match the black and red twist pattern on the top portion of my dress. My eyes found Ms. Decker talking to a group of older women. I made my way through the crowd and walked close enough to overhear Ms. Decker express her gratitude for having the opportunity to teach. Ms. Decker waved her right hand in a short, quick inward movement motioning for me to join them, but middle-aged woman was standing between Ms. Decker and I.

"Excuse me, Ma'am," I said politely.

The woman obliged and moved aside as she said,

"You look pretty this evening young lady."

I responded with a bigger smile and said, "Thank you, Ma'am."

There were others who smiled or nodded at me in approval of how I presented myself. I took pride in the way I was being raised.

When I stepped into the group, Ms. Decker stopped what she was doing and gave me a warm hug. She put both of her hands on my shoulders, leaned back with a smile and said, "Wow, young lady, you look beautiful!" They started laughing and Ms. Decker began to introduce me to her colleagues. "Joan is the principle of a high school; she's been nominated for the Humanitarian Award. If you ever need good ideas on where to find volunteer work in the community, she's very resourceful." Ms. Decker turned her attention to Joan and said, "And this is Brenda. She's one of my 'A' students at St. Paul on the West side of Chicago. She's here with Savar, Devon and Valerie. They're all future leaders and athletes in the community. You know I'm a big believer in supporting our youth. These young people have so much potential and so much to offer, I have to keep an eye on them."

Joan responded, "Lydia, you're such a youth preserver. I like the fact that you always set an example by bringing the best youth to the forefront and give them an example of what they can achieve. And welcome Brenda, you look remarkable!" She reached for my hand and I reciprocated.

"Thank you, Ms. Joan, I appreciate it," I replied.

"This young lady is even articulate." Joan turned back to me and responded, "You're very welcome Brenda. I hope you enjoy the ceremony and have a spectacular time." Joan eventually stopped shaking my hand and released her grip. Joan gestured for me to go into the ballroom as she and Ms. Decker continued their conversation. I nodded and smiled graciously before heading into the ballroom.

The tables had small, stainless steel labels on them. Each round table was covered with a red velvet tablecloth and included black signs with the host name. I spotted Ms. Decker's sign. As I walked toward the table, I noticed the glistening light from the six-foot wide gothic chandelier above me. The room was decorated with various congratulatory remarks such as "Leadership is the key," "Inspire and create new leaders," and "Congratulations on your philanthropic achievement!" There were so many positive citations throughout the room, hanging from the ceiling, standing on oversized easels and the corners of the ballroom. An instrumental version of Earth, Wind and Fire's, "Hearts of Fire" played through Yamaha speakers positioned throughout the room. It made me feel older and more significant.

For the last three weeks, Devon and I had been talking on the phone almost every day for hours. I knew I'd recognize him. My mind jumped back to when I went through the mail and hid the phone bill so my Mom wouldn't see all the long distance calls made to North Chicago. When I opened the bill, I knew it would be unusually high, but two hundred dollars was a shock to me! My intention was to work extra hours and pay it off before anybody could find out. In the meantime, I hid it in my Lipstick Allí shoebox and tucked it in a corner underneath my bed. His English diction and articulation were perfect. When Devon spoke, I could close my eyes and picture each story like a movie. He didn't simply describe how he felt or say what was on his mind; he was expressive, used examples and past experiences of his or others to communicate his point. I found it to be an attractive characteristic.

During all of our telephone conversations, I felt as if I was talking to someone older because he sounded intelligent. I was sixteen and he was a year and a half older than me when we first began to speak on the phone. Ms. Decker always spoke highly of Devon when she referenced her brother either in the classroom or in private discussions. They lived in the same house with their mom in North Chicago, Illinois. When Ms. Decker taught, she rented a condominium near the West side and the association flipped the bill.

Devon taught me about the politics that existed behind the Vietnam War and how they not only messed up the location by going there to fight, but crippled their own too. He read Zora Neal Hurston's literature and Afeni Shakur's articles at the age of seventeen. He was a boy with an unusually mature heart; like a man. His voice was pure and soft, almost like a falsetto, but riddled with passion. A smile spread across my face at the thought of him.

I snapped back to reality as I began to walk closer to the assigned table and noticed a gorgeous young man with golden brown skin and dimples standing and looking in my direction. His hair was neatly cut and tightly curled; he had perfect white teeth and was tall for a seventeen-year-old. When I reached the table, he extended his right hand and gently pulled me close. He softly clutched my small waist in his arms. He looked at me while he cuddled me in the folds of his arms. I returned the gentle embrace. I didn't feel desperation from the heat generating from his body, but genuinely felt like this was a much-needed moment because we had been anticipating it for months. Devon gave me a friendly kiss on the cheek. I felt comfortable with my arms locked around him.

The moment was nothing like the dance or kiss I had with Junior during my birthday party. This experience was overwhelmed with emotion, which was a first for me. At first sight, I knew I'd learn about love through Devon. "Wow, you look just as I imagined you would. Delicate, innocent and you smell delicious," Devon whispered as he smiled. I looked down at his black Stacy Adams, then at his purple and white bow tie and smelled a scent that I absolutely loved. He smelled like Mustafa, the most exotic and manliest of men.

I responded with a calm tone to elude sounding nervous, "Thanks Devon. It's great to finally be face-to-face with you. And you look really handsome in your suit. You're a lot taller than what I thought you'd be." Devon had this smirk on his face that led me to feel as if he wanted to surprise me with certain aspects about himself. When we spoke over the phone, I'd ask about his height, but he'd always respond with comments like, "I'm average" or "I'm tall enough." He knew that one of my favorite things about a guy was height. I didn't prefer short guys, not because there is anything wrong with it, but when I wore heels, I felt uncomfortable if I was taller.

Devon pulled the velvet cherry wood chair away from the table and motioned with his hand for me to sit. I straightened my dress so that the back wouldn't wrinkle as I sat down. He scooted the chair forward from behind me so I was comfortably seated in front of my flat wear setting. The crowd outside of the ballroom began to stroll into the award decorated dinning area and before we knew it, the room was full of conversation and chatter. Devon and I still amazed with each other, discussed the NAACP and how grateful we were to join the celebration.

Devon talked about how adamant his sister is about supporting community improvement and education for those that are disenfranchised. I spotted Ms. Decker making her way to the table. She made eye contact with me and knew that Devon had already introduced himself. After the audience settled in, a roaring applause erupted as Roy Wilkins took to the stage to deliver the introduction for the evening. My attention shifted from Ms. Decker and Devon to the stage as the event officially began.

CHAPTER 2
EDUCATION ON LOVE

My impression of Devon was that he wanted to be with me. The evening at the NAACP ceremony had confirmed that. The sixty-mile distance we lived apart from each other didn't stop us. I felt that I wasn't the most beautiful girl in my class nor in the Chicago area I grew up in. I knew there were flirtatious girls who were probably more promiscuous than I could even imagine. However, I didn't doubt that he and I had a connection. Devon and I talked a lot and explored the "what if's" because it helped us get to know each other and what we liked. He and I were more mature for our age, but we were still young and dreamers. We imagined what it would be like to be in a band together. I'd write the music and play the drums while he played classical piano because he knew instrumental patterns and could navigate a soundboard. We pretended that we were casting auditions for the best singers for our backup studio sessions. I picked Diana Ross, Marlon Jackson and Ray Parker Jr. to be in our group sessions while he chose Chaka Khan, Elton John and Jody Watley. We would sing songs to each other and judge the quality then pick the lead singer and the background singers. Even though Devon and I couldn't see each other in person, we would both lie on the sofa in our living room or stretch out on the floor and continue talking.

Devon's presence and warmth was real and reassuring to me. It was the time he spent with me doing random things that persuaded me to believe I was loved. Devon wrote me poems that I always kept.

> *What is beautiful within cannot be denied*
> *When I see you, I see the beauty within*
> *What is soft and fragile,*
> *please touch gently and be kind*
> *When I see you, I see you kissing me softly*
> *What is loud and rambunctious, is an interruption of my concentration on our quiet walks in the park and the whisper of words that describe why you are my radiant sunshine.*

Devon sent me poems on special occasions. Typically, it was when I did well in my basketball games, aced an exam or when he wanted to remind me that he was thinking of me. Since I lived on the West side of Chicago and he lived ninety minutes away in North Chicago, he would mail them to me. I kept all twelve of them in my Lipstick Allí box. He knew I looked forward to receiving mail from him so he'd fold them like origami requiring me to be patient. When I was with Devon, close and from afar, I felt at home.

Being home is a feeling of security in a loving environment. I grew up in a nice home but I felt something was missing when I began to spend time with Devon. Devon always talked about love and was very humble and compassionate. He was all over me. I don't say that in a negative way, but because I was unaccustomed to hearing "I love you" all the time and having someone cater to me in a personal way. I didn't exactly grow up hearing those words, hugging, kissing and displaying affection. My parents displayed the niceties and I know they loved each other. Regardless, I never saw them openly show affectionate with each other. I thought that was normal. It didn't bother me at all until I had someone in my life exude love and affection as easily as a handshake. Grace was the best way to describe Devon's actions towards me. What I found difficult was reciprocating. I didn't know how to exhibit that love and passion for him the way he expressed it so freely towards me.

Devon's whole family was openly passionate about life and everything else. I could hear his mom say things like, "Devon, baby, give your mama a hug and kiss. I'm leaving for work." Even while I was on the phone I could hear their exchange of kisses and affection. I found it a bit surprising and foreign, but he told me that his dad was the same way. Their philosophy was that if something happened to either of them and by the grace of God, nothing would, their kids would remember their last loving exchange with one another. I have no doubt that my parents truly loved and would do anything for us, but when it came to openly demonstrating affection, the house was quiet. But when I spent time with Devon, I could see and feel the difference between the free spirit of displaying love and affection within his family and the quiet assumptions within mine. My kiss with Junior was the first physical sensation I felt with a male. But my experiences with Devon were emotional and arousing.

Christian and I fought hard as brother and sister, but we were still best friends. He enjoyed playing softball and racing cars with me. He was at an impressionable stage of his life. Christian wanted to do everything I did, including playing the drums, riding bikes and playing in the band. We had secrets, but sometimes when we fought, he would start crying and then run to tell Mom on me. It wasn't often, but depending on the situation I was grounded or spanked. I know Christian loved me, but for some reason, he felt like he was my equal and could argue toe-to-toe. We always made up after fights and he was my only baby brother. I trusted him, but resented his curiosity of my personal business. Christian helped himself to my things and all I wanted him to do was grow into his own and mind his business instead of mine.

One time, I was grounded for locking Christian in the garage for hours because he took my bike for a ride. But the next day, I snuck out to visit Devon; and I took Christian with me. **Christian and I typically made up after our fights and he promised he wouldn't tell Mom that I took him to North Chicago so I could visit Devon. It was on a Saturday morning when Mom told me to watch Christian because she had to work a double shift. I put my hand over the telephone receiver, looked up at her with a smile and said that I would. I proceeded to tell Devon my version of why I was grounded. We'd been talking on the phone for nearly thirty-minutes at that point. Devon said he had an idea, but he asked that I listen before responding or making a decision.

"I overheard your mom say that she was leaving and you mentioned that being grounded meant you couldn't do your usual things. So take the train and come visit me."

I paused for a brief moment, and then moved the phone away from my mouth calling out, "Christian, put on a pair of jeans, a sweater and tennis shoes. We're going out." I could almost see Devon smiling through the telephone. He new the train times to and from North Chicago. The weather in Chicago was mild; there was no sign of winter. Temperatures were still mild resting in the sixty-five to seventy degree range. I was comfortable in my Lee blue jeans, a white cotton sweater and loafers. It cost a dollar fifty each to ride the CTA bus to the Amtrak Train Station. Christian and I played Gin Rummy during the entire hour and a half train ride. The ride seemed to take forever because I was excited to see Devon. We hadn't seen each other for almost three months since the NAACP event in August. I was thinking about how natural love was verses being demanding. That's what I learned from Devon. I knew when choosing someone to be with, I should never lower my standards.

Waukegan was located between Chicago and Milwaukee. It was a diverse town of about seventy-five thousand people and had a thriving lakefront with the most picturesque residential communities one could imagine. It was definitely a growing middle class area. The last Amtrak stop was downtown Waukegan. As the train slowed towards the platform, Christian and I gathered our things and stood up. When the train came to a stop, we exited through the doors and began to walk towards the end of the platform. Devon said he'd meet us at the Grand Ave. exit but I didn't see him in the small crowd of people. Christian and I walked down the stairs to the front entrance on Grand Ave. The station was busy with families and businessmen leaving their taxis with brief cases or luggage ready for today's travel.

I looked at the yellow cabs and black Sedan's lined-up in a long row along Grand Ave. Then, I spotted Devon standing in front of the left passenger door of one of the black Sedan's. He had a grin on his face, but I could see his sparkling white teeth as the grin spread into a full fledge smile as we made eye contact. Devon had on a pair of Levi blue jeans with a black cardigan sweater and black loafers. He was holding the door open waiting for us. Christian and I started toward the car. Devon approached us, grabbed my hand and leaned in to give me a kiss on the cheek. He looked down at Christian and said, "Hello young man, I'm Devon, how are you?" Christian was holding my right hand, but let go to greet Devon with a handshake.

"Hi, I'm Christian. Is that your car?" I could see the excitement spread across his face. "This is awesome!"

Devon responded, "It's great to meet you Christian, and no it's not mine; it's like a cab. My family wanted to make sure you guys were comfortable. Come on, let's get out of here." Devon opened the door for us to climb inside and he sat in the front.

Christian was happy to be on an adventure and didn't ask questions about where we were going. For the most part, he was good at keeping secrets when I asked him because he knew that I would take him places, too. Devon and I had a plan. Christian could play with Devon's cousin, Evan, while we spent time together. Evan was nine years old, one year younger than Christian. He was sitting in the back seat as we all settled in.

Evan introduced himself, "Hey, I'm Evan. I guess you and I are hanging out today, huh?"

"Yeah, sweet," Christian replied.

Christian and Evan continued to get to know one another while Devon told the driver to head home.

The house was only a fifteen-minute drive from the Amtrak train station. The driver pulled in front of the house and Devon handed him a ten-dollar bill while the three of us got out of the car. I gazed at the medium-sized, two-story brick home with a black rod iron fence wrapped around it. The house had a wraparound porch and a detached two-car garage. We walked through the backyard onto the cobblestone sidewalk, which led to the back door entrance. Devon led the way up the stairs into the enclosed back porch with large screened windows around it. Two Havana dark, seagrass chairs and matching ottomans were set up around a tempered glass-top coffee table. It made the porch look cozy and peaceful.

"This is really beautiful, Devon."

He had a huge grin on his face as he turned around and said, "Thanks, baby girl." He turned back around and continued, "Mom is the best decorator. She likes the seagrass type of seats. It's really cool; it's like the woven material." Devon turned the key in the lock and pushed down on the handle to open the door. We entered through the kitchen, which was small, but immaculate and everything looked new. The appliances were sparkling white and the stove had a griddle in the center. As we walked through the kitchen, I noticed ham and turkey sandwiches and a macaroni pasta salad on the counter wrapped in cling wrap.

"Mom prepared lunch before she left to run a couple errands."

"Oh, thank you. I'm pretty hungry and Christian probably is by now, too." Once we put our backpacks away, everyone washed their hands. Devon poured lemonade; we blessed the food and ate lunch.

Evan and Christian couldn't wait to pull out all of the toys so they went downstairs to the basement. The visit was full of energy, we were laughing and talking. Christian and Evan connected immediately and appeared to be inseparable. Devon and I both knew this was our opportunity to spend time together. We were like magnets and hard to separate.

At the age of sixteen and seventeen, we both had the typical yearning and curiosity about love, sex and passion. He and I ventured off to the den, which was a small room in the corner of the house. It had big wooden blinds, dark brown hardwood floors and a leather loveseat with an oversized quilt throw on it. We sat on the loveseat smiling as we looked into each other's eyes. Devon slid over a brown box with his album collection inside. We both loved music, so we pulled out the album covers and talked about our favorite songs and groups. Earth Wind and Fire, Diana Ross, Sky, Shalamar, The Jackson 5, The Carpenters, Average White Band, and The Isely Brothers. There was a Panasonic record player and speakers on a small, oak wood stand in the corner of the den. Devon put on "Boogie Wonderland," held out his hand and said to me, "Lets dance, Brenda."

Devon and I danced to a fast two-step and held hands. He had a stoic seriousness about him when he danced which seemed deliberate. I could see his throat moving slightly as he whispered the words of the song. Out of pure exhaustion, we plopped back down on the leather loveseat. I shifted my position so I was leaning against him while he rested his back on the cushioned pillows. He stroked his fingers through the front on my bangs and I listened to him hum the songs as the rest of the album played.

I felt Devon's heart beating and his sweet breath trickling the back of my neck. Lying in his arms felt so natural and warm. He was seventeen, but had an old spirit. He shared how much he missed me since we last saw one another at the NAACP dinner.

"Baby girl, I love talking to you on the phone, but it feels right with you here, closer to me. I want us to be together. Maybe I can transfer schools," he said softly. Before I could respond, he leaned down, kissed my neck and left a trail of kisses up to my ear. He made his way to my cheek and then I felt his soft, beautiful lips touch mine. We grew silent because we were entirely consumed with one another.

As we continued to kiss, I felt his fingers slowly unbutton the top three buttons of my crewneck sweater. The scuffling sound of the turntable needle on the Earth, Wind and Fire album was the only sound filling the room. I pulled away from a deep penetrating kiss and sat up to button my sweater back up. "Devon, it'll scratch the album if we don't fix it. Besides, we have to check on Christian and Evan."

Devon got up and headed for the bathroom down the hall while I found my way to the basement. I opened the door and called out to the boys, "Are you guys okay down there?"

I heard laughing before they responded in unison, "We're good!" As I headed back to the den, Devon opened the bathroom door and pulled me into his warm embrace. He placed a simple kiss on my lips and then stared into my eyes for what seemed like forever. It was beautiful.

After that day, Devon and I had several more secretive meetings like this. He would conveniently offer to babysit his cousin Evan while his mom and aunt attended events and his dad traveled for work. I saved my train tickets in my Lipstick Allí box because he always wrote, "I love Devon" on the back of my tickets.

Christian never told Mom about his adventures to Waukegan, IL. I realized how much of a risk-taker I had become. Devon was the first young man I truly fell in love with. The love and respect he showed me set the standard for all men as I embarked on the world as a young lady in college and as a woman.

After high school, he joined the Air Force and traveled overseas. I moved to Minnesota to attend College at Augsburg University and then transferred to the University of Minnesota to study Journalism and Communications. As I moved through different phases of my life, I thought of Devon, as well as, Ms. Decker. They helped me to develop and understand my deeper, inner self. While my love for Devon eventually faded as life kicked into full force, I did encounter a similar experience later that changed me into the person I am today.

CHAPTER 3
HIS ABSENCE

My Dad passed away when I was eleven-years-old. He battled cancer and it defeated him. But a few years prior to his death, Mom spent most of her time caring for him when she wasn't working at the post office. What I remember most about this time were the frequent visits to the hospital. Although my Dad was a strong man he couldn't fight the illness and the chemotherapy took a toll on him. There were times when he was able to come home and enjoy familiar surroundings. However, most of his time was spent in bed with my mom administering his medicine, making him soup and helping him through his incessant coughing spasms. During this time, our house remained melancholy and quiet because we all knew that Dad wasn't doing well. Other family would visit and help in anyway possible. It was painful to watch my Dad suffer the way he did and he fought for several months.

The last time Dad returned to the hospital, he needed to have a second surgery. The first surgery was done to remove a tumor in his leg and during the procedure the doctors discovered Dad had Cancer. The second surgery was done to evaluate what was growing inside his lungs. The cancer relentlessly spread to the rest of his organs. When the surgeons closed him up and completed the surgery, they knew that there was nothing more that could be done. A few months later, I found Mom in her bedroom alone. I peeped in and saw her hand and arm resting on the wood board siding of her closet door with her head leaned inside of the closet. The only thing visible was her arm. It was in the morning time and Mom only wore her house robe. The sleeve of her blue robe sagged down her arm. I walked over to her and noticed that she was crying. I grabbed her by her waist and asked what was wrong. She said, "Your Dad has passed away." Mom and I walked over to the bed and sat down in silence. The only thing I could do at that time was to offer her a Kleenex.

    I felt numb and at the age of eleven, I didn't understand what I was feeling. It wasn't until a week later at the funeral, that I truly understood what the future held. I was living in the black without my Dad because cancer had ravished him until there was nothing left. He no longer looked like the handsome young confident and strong man that he was. Instead, his appearance was limp, sunken and drawn inward. His skin was shriveled and dark and he looked thirty years older than his tender age of thirty-seven. I fell into a dark emotional hole of sadness and confusion because Dad's death was sudden. I felt as if I hadn't built the close relationship that I should have with him. And I realized that I still needed him. The void that resulted contributed to the reason I struggled with giving affection in my own personal relationships.

    Mom, Teri, Christian and I managed to keep a normal schedule and lifestyle after my Dad's passing. Mom worked more hours at the post office. Teri, Christian and I increased our responsibilities with chores around the house. We were already used to the feeling of Dad not being home because prior to his death, he was in and out of the hospital for about two years. The emptiness at home felt the same but the fact that he would never return home caused the three of us to lean more heavily on Mom for emotional support and continued guidance. We had to keep moving because life did so. After many condolences from family neighbors and church members, things slowly returned to normal. Christian was only five at the time and didn't seem to be affected as much as Teri and I. He knew Dad wouldn't be around to play with him or take him to the park, but Mom asked me to entertain him more often.

We didn't know what to do other than pitch in and step up to make things a little easier for Mom. Terri was mature and sensitive to Mom needing help with keeping the house in order and she stepped in more as a leader while Mom worked. I hid my grief by staying busy with basketball or just suppressing my feelings all together. I saw how much she was hurting and I wanted to protect Mom and do whatever I could to make her happy. I refused to walk around the house in a somber mood. I'd smile and try to manage sustaining a positive attitude as best I could because I knew it would make Mom happy.

Mom's friend Josie tried to keep her happy as well. Josie was a loud bodacious woman who attended Church with us on Sunday. She wore a brunette wig and lots of make-up. I really liked her variety of leather coats. She always wore a different color with fur around the collar. Her leather coats matched personality. Josie was always smiling and she talked loudly. She would visit regularly and convince mom to go out to play cards or join her at a steppers dance show. I could tell that Josie made mom feel better because she started smiling and laughing more and whenever she would hang out with Josie, she seemed happy. My mom was a homebody and rarely socialized unless she was hosting a bid-wiz card game or a Church event.

One day, Josie introduced my mom to Tate Sherman. Tate was a sharp dresser and always looked rather sporty. He wore tinted classes and nice sweaters, similar to Mr. Bill Cosby. He was a blue-collar worker with a small afro and a dose of swagger. I noticed that he was very affection with Mom. And because Josie couldn't bear to think of her friend as a single young widow with three children, she insisted that Mom needed a good man. I thought Tate was cool and as long as he treated my mother well and kept her happy I was in agreement.

Tate grew on me over time, but he wasn't the prime example of a father figure like my Dad. Instead of giving direction and leading the household, he sat back and observed. He just became a part of it. He didn't embrace my brother, Christian as a young boy that needed a man to help him develop; he ignored him as though it wasn't his role. However, I appreciated the fact that Tate catered to my mother and lavished her with gifts and kisses. Although all of us missed Dad, Tate's affection was exactly what she needed at that point. I noticed Tate seemed to just love my Mom. I never felt his affection towards me. In some strange way, I needed to hear my stepdad say that he loved me too and sometimes, I needed a hug.

As time went by and Tate's relationship evolved with my mother and things changed a bit when he moved in and we became one big happy family.

There was only one thing missing, the part about family. Tate still never made an effort to express the love I thought a parent should when he was about to have an extended family of three young children. I never felt protected or loved by him and that was something I had with my Dad and needed with him too. Eventually, Tate said he loved me, but by that time, I was accustomed to not expecting it.

We visited six flags and Niagara Falls enjoying our time together, but I felt a distinct separation between Tate and Mom Teri, Christian and I.

At an early point in my life I developed a perception of what I thought family was. I considered real family time to encompass, watching a movie together and discuss the plot to share thoughts. It was supposed to bring about open communication and opportunities to learn from one another. Growing as a family includes having dinner together every night and discussing the details of your day. Authentic family time brings the family together for cooking, cleaning and getting down on your knees to pray together.

Our structure changed and Mom served Tate dinner in the living room on most days while we ate in the kitchen. We watched movies in separate rooms because Tate smoked cigarettes and I couldn't stomach the smoke. I never saw Tate in the kitchen helping Mom prepare a meal, nor did I ever see him in the kitchen helping clean it. Since he didn't participate in those activities, there wasn't any leadership from him with regard to prayer either.

CHAPTER 4
MEETING CEDRIC

From 1990 through 1991, serial killer Jeffrey Dahmer was arrested for the deaths of seventeen boys and men. Magic Johnson tested positive for HIV then retired from the NBA to become a spokesperson for HIV and AIDS awareness and education. Rodney King was shown on national television being brutally kicked and beaten by four police officers in Los Angeles, California. Police reports were leaked about a Supreme Court nominee, Clarence Thomas, who was being accused of sexual harassment by a woman who worked for him ten years prior. Princess Diana and Prince Charles decided to end their royal marriage. On August 6, 1991 the worldwide web became available and changed how we communicated. The events began to unfold and more tension infiltrated the world.

My favorite Aunt Cece gave me the book, "I Dream a World" by Brian Lanker and Maya Angelou. The book included portraits of seventy-five African American women who changed the world by dreaming big and using their talents to become pioneers of America in their own unique way. Aunt Cece always thought I was special and told me that I would make my mark in some way. I read the profiles of the beautiful legends in that book and I am still amazed at how many women have endured, persevered and achieved so much despite their obstacles. Aunt Cece gave me this book on June 29th, 1989.

I was a proud and professional thirty-year-old woman. I had a condo in the Warehouse District, which was one of the affluent downtown communities. I had earned a college degree and was a pharmaceutical sales representative. After many years of the socialite life, which included dating white boys, traveling and being single, my mission was to find a good black man. I didn't discriminate when it came to finding love, but my career was at its peek and all I wanted was true love. It seemed like the older I got, the fainter my love lessons with Devon became. What intrigued me about the white men I dated at this time was their generosity and curiosity about life. I was tired of the dating scene and like many other single women; I wanted to settle down. I prayed that I would meet a decent man, someone that would encourage and inspire me. On that same day, that next year, Cedric and I met in downtown Minneapolis.

When I spent the night out on the town, I typically attended events with my close friends, Lisa and David. They always knew about the hotspots in town and if there was a place or event, they had VIP tickets or hosted the gathering. However, this particular night was different. Instead of spending the evening with other couples, I decided to go alone to the Perimeter Nightclub. Perimeter was a multi-layered chic dance and jazz club. There was always good thumping music, a great ambiance and delicious food. It was a well-known establishment for media enthusiasts, professional athletes and local artists.

Whenever I spent a night out, I always hoped to meet someone special. If I had to pick a place for it to happen, it would be there. The dance floor was circular with an old wooden floor, similar to a dance studio. Upstairs on the roof was the jazz loft. Nic's jazz quartet was playing Kenny G's "Midnight Motion." The main floor was spacious with high ceilings and oversized windows on each wall. The windowpanes were large and made of cedar wood.

Each room had its distinct look and unique theme. The main floor included an oversized circular marble bar with matching swivel chairs. The lower level was packed with all types of people. This was the perfect environment to have a cocktail, mingle and enjoy the sound of "Get a Life" by Soul II Soul. The great thing about R&B in the '90s was that it included every emotion imaginable. "This is How We Do It," "Get off," "Poison," and "All Around the World" were classics. Perimeter was a refurbished old train depot located in the Warehouse District. It was original, quaint and big enough to comfortably hold about two hundred people for dinner, jazz or dancing. I chatted with a few acquaintances and snacked on crab cakes and chicken wings. The food was cooked to order and was served steaming hot.

I definitely enjoyed the styles of dancing. I wasn't ashamed to participate in krumping, roger rabbit and the electric slide. As I finished my appetizers and began to make my way closer to the dance floor, I heard a voice behind me say, "Excuse me lovely lady, would you like to dance?" I turned around to see a six-foot-two gorgeous man. His coffee creamed complexion was as smooth as butter. He had thick black eyebrows with matching mesmerizing oval dark brown eyes. Cedric's nose and mouth matched someone of Cuban descent; not too broad and not to slender. He wore a manicured haircut that displayed a quarter of an inch of his thick black curly hair. He was dressed in a white, button down starched shirt and pleated blue slacks. He wore a pair of black *Jo Ghost* dress shoes. I loved a tall, good-looking man with quality shoes because it's an indication that he pays attention to details and can take care of himself.

When I looked back up, he was smiling beautifully while awaiting my response. I returned the smile and placed my hand in his, accepting his invitation to proceeded to the dance floor. After almost an hour, we stepped off the floor and went to another section of the main floor to have a more private talk. The lighting was dim, adding a bit of intimacy to the tranquil atmosphere. He was extremely courteous and appeared to be a natural gentleman. He pulled my chair away from the table and pushed the chair in when I sat down. He held out his hand and formally introduced himself, "My name's Cedric."

I shook his hand and responded, "Nice to meet you Cedric, I'm Brenda."

"I saw you cross my path and I couldn't pass up dancing with you."

"Well, I'm glad you took a chance and asked me."

Amidst the music and scores of people there was an immediate connection and attraction between us. Cedric had a gentle and charming presence. He appeared to have a peaceful nature, but there was something underlying that was somewhat firm or demanding. He was quite articulate and professional which told me he was comfortable expressing himself. He was knowledgeable about politics and was well informed of many topics of discussion. He talked about various renovation projects around Minneapolis and then I learned that he owned a construction company. Both of us had successful jobs and managed to make time to take care of our physical appearances.

He was born in Nashville, Tennessee and grew up in a Pentecostal family as the youngest of nine children. He mentioned that his parents were strict, consistently enforcing principles and rules. It seemed as if he had a solid upbringing. Although his family had their challenges, they stayed together. He lightheartedly joked about when his childhood. He said when he was a kid; he had to compete with his brothers and sisters for the last piece of chicken at the dinner table.

I explained, "After my dad passed away years ago, Mom didn't marry again. My mom met a man that she thought she would marry. I called him Stepdad because I thought so, too. They lived together for over fifteen years and then one day, he just left."

While Cedric spoke, my eyes somberly dropped to the floor and I thought about what it would have been like to have both of my parents at this point in my life. I missed them tremendously.

I thought he and I complimented each other in many ways. I was a little talkative and energetic, but it was because I truly enjoyed his company. I couldn't take my eyes off of him during the entire evening and he didn't leave my side. For hours, it felt like everything around us was at a standstill and our attention was uninterrupted.

Our engaging conversation caused me to have a deep interest in Cedric but as the night progressed, we noticed the crowd had begun to dissipate. Eventually, Cedric and I realized the Perimeter was preparing to close so we headed for the exit. Patrons slowly began to congregate outside and flag down valet attendants to retrieve their vehicles. It was midsummer in Minneapolis and the air was refreshing. The bright stars illuminated the dark sky beautifully. Cedric walked me to my car and graciously asked if I would join him for breakfast in the morning. Before I answered, my body elevated to match his height and my lips locked onto his. Cedric's hands firmly grasped my waist and pulled me closer; I could feel his intense passion. Trying to compose myself, I reached into my purse to find one of my business cards. "Call me in the morning and let me know when and where."

Cedric took the card, glanced at it and said, "I definitely will."

That was a great beginning to a relationship in my mind. After learning more about him, I knew I wanted him. I wanted to be respectful and not expose myself too soon. After staring into his eyes, I said, "I have to go now. But I look forward to seeing you tomorrow for breakfast."

I turned to open my car door when he cut in, "Oh, could you give me a ride to my car? It's parked four blocks away."

I quickly responded, "Of course. That's not a problem." Cedric walked around to the passenger side, opened the door and climbed in. We put on our seatbelt and I started the car. When I glanced over, he was staring at me. "So, which way is your car?"

"Sorry. It's parked on the corner of First and Maple Ave." I drove four blocks down the road and he pointed to a black car parked next to the curb. Before he got out of the car, he leaned over and gently kissed my right cheek. Then he opened the door and was gone.

I shifted gears and began to head home. When I looked in the rearview mirror, I could see his car disappear in the other direction. My prayers had been answered. I pulled into the driveway, turned off the ignition and opened the door. When the car light came on, I went to reach for my purse, but noticed one of my cards lying on the passenger seat.

CHAPTER 5
THE DREAM

By the time I arrived home it was shortly after midnight. After a long exhausting yawn, I rubbed my eyes, dropped my purse on the sofa and went into my bedroom. What a long day, I just wanted to climb into my bed and sink into a deep sleep but it seemed like my mind kept racing. I went into the bathroom and turned on the shower. Thoughtlessly, I slipped off my clothes and jumped into a hot shower. Ten minutes later I was putting on my pajamas and diving comfortably into bed. I'm sure I was still glowing as I thought about how blessed I was to have met Cedric. I laid on my pillow and faced the ceiling with my hands locked behind my head. My smile wouldn't go away as that night replayed in my head. I seem to drift a little deeper with each rising thought. The way Cedric described his parents made them appear as if they were the sweetest couple ever. Although they both had a few health challenges in their '60s and raised nine children, they still called each other "Babe." He described his mom as a short and stout woman with a beautiful smile. She respected and looked up to Cedric who had admirable qualities and was well spoken, knowledgeable and openly expressed his faith. Two of his brothers were pastors in the Nashville, Tennessee area. Since I was in such a good place in my thoughts, I tried to stay awake for a bit longer, but I could feel myself being pulled into a deep sleep so I surrendered.

Cedric and I sat across from my Mom and Dad who were in their late '60s. My parents had been married for over thirty-five years and truly loved each other. Mom loved being around people and would always entertain friends and family on the weekends. They would play bid-wiz, spades or go bowling when the mood struck. Dad occasionally joined in, but he seemed to like watching his wife enjoy herself more. The couples met for hours and talked about their lives and common interests. This included places they traveled to, people, raising kids and managing in the world, as it was so different from when they were young adults.

Cedric's parents and mine sat down and evaluated us to see if we'd be a good fit together. Initially, there was a light debate between our parents. They displayed a bit of tension and concern over our developing relationship. My parents wanted me to have the absolute best. They had some doubts because they wanted to ensure that Cedric would be a loving husband, good provider and potentially a dedicated father. Cedric's parents adored me, but were uneasy for a different reason. They thought I was too dedicated to my career and wanted me to be more of a homemaker.

Every third Friday for the next six months, they met up to discuss how Cedric and I grew up and our individual values that were instilled at an early age. Both **my parents and Cedric's parents had different philosophies on marriage. Regardless of how hard they tried, they couldn't seem to agree.**

However, after long consideration, both sides settled on Cedric and I becoming united in marriage. I was ecstatic and found myself jumping up and down for joy when my parents gave me the news. But in an instant, the room suddenly became as dark as night and ominous. Unexpectedly, I was hesitant about Cedric and I felt like I was failing to see the whole picture; I was missing something important because I was only seeing what I wanted.

I woke up abruptly with my heart racing. My dream was vivid and felt real, but it was bizarre. It's normal for a person to have up to seven dreams in one night. The REM sleep stage lasts for sixty to ninety minutes and then repeats itself during the course of the night. I believe in the theory that dreams not only reflect our life experiences, but echo our concerns, too. I continuously dreamt of many different meetings like this, but I didn't read too much into them. I looked to the left and glanced at the clock on my nightstand. I realized that I had overslept a bit. I sat up and stretched, thinking about what I had planned for the day.

I turned the nozzle on, undressed and stepped into the steamy shower. I felt something deep in my core for Cedric and believed that he could be an exceptional man, but I still needed to get to know him further. I couldn't help but notice a feeling of familiarity. After turning the water off, I grabbed one of my towels, dried myself and got dressed. I put on a nice, but casual fitted blue blouse, a pair of jeans and black sandals. I walked into the living room, turned on the morning news and lounged around my condominium, waiting to hear from Cedric about where to meet him for breakfast.

Time passed and I thought that I would have heard from Cedric by now. I glanced at my watch a couple of times wondering if he'd uphold his commitment. Suddenly, the bellman's voice came through my intercom announced on my intercom that there was a visitor downstairs. I left my unit feeling both curious and excited that it could be Cedric. I walked down the hallway, entered the freight elevator and pressed the lobby button. When the elevator stopped and opened, I could see a glimpse of him sitting in one of the lounge chairs.

"Good morning, Cedric. Wow, I figured you would have called first."

"Hey lovely lady. I'm sorry; I lost your card but remembered the last five digits of your phone number. I looked at every number in the phone book and when I found one that looked familiar, I gave it a shot. I was hoping to surprise you." Cedric smiled and pulled me towards him to hug me. Suddenly, I realized the card that was left on the passenger seat last night was his. His dedication to find me proved that I wasn't the only one who felt the amazing connection between us.

Cedric drove us to Sidney's to have breakfast. We devoured Belgian waffles, savory apple bacon, freshly squeezed orange juice and gourmet coffee. The conversation between us was interesting and engaging. We talked about the previous night and how comfortable we felt with one other. As well, we opened up about past relationships and goals for the future. I made it clear that I would remain celibate until I found the right man to marry. Cedric amazingly obliged and didn't appear threaten by my principles in the least bit. He responded, "Well, we'll just get married then!" After that morning, Cedric and I officially began seeing each other frequently. When we attended gatherings with friends and colleagues, we always shared the story of how we met.

CHAPTER 6
THE SIGNS

    Cedric and I became inseparable and we were seen everywhere together. For my job, I was required to attend HealthCare speaking engagements as well as community events. There were opportunities to meet and greet local officials, attend gala affairs, business dinners and stay well connected. Cedric was always by my side. Our friends weren't unanimous on their feelings about us as a couple and we knew they had their doubts. In particular, my friends wondered if Cedric could handle my high maintenance style. But, they seemed envious because Cedric always captivated anyone he engaged in a conversation with. Part of his personality was that he was extremely candid and approachable. He was knowledgeable about current events and was politically astute. Bottom line, Cedric was the life of the party. He had that subtle and luminous radiation about him.

    After dating for a little while, there was a slight shift in the way things had been going. Cedric was down on his luck as far as employment. He took a job as a loan officer in between trying to secure a big contract with a condo complex on the west side of town. He was solid with numbers and a perfectionist. His skill set with his construction business included analytics, calculating dimensions and project management so his position as a loan officer was a familiar one. Additionally, Cedric worked in the banking industry five years prior to starting his construction business. This was a temporary position to make ends meet until his contract was finalized.

Over the years, the industry involved a more automated computer dependent system. However, Cedric wasn't efficient with the processing system on computers and struggled in that aspect. The stress negatively impacted him greatly. Likewise, he felt pressured because the housing market was booming at this time and dependent on loan officers.

Kendal and Cedric were old college buddies who remained close friends through the years. Kendal made a career of being a loan officer after graduating from college. He worked at a different location than Cedric, but they occasionally met for lunch.

Kendal was quiet, collected and professional. He was the type of guy who could spend all day in a garage fixing and tinkering with cars, then walk into the office and confidently run a business meeting. He was definitely versatile and had many talents. Kendal became a mutual friend of mine just as Lisa and David got to know Cedric. He was one of few friends who knew a different side of Cedric that I had not yet seen. One day, Kendal called and expressed a bit of trepidation.

After quite a few rings, I picked up the phone in a hurry and said, "Hello?"

"Hey, how's everything going?"

"Oh, hey, Kendal," I said, slightly caught off guard. "Everything's great. Thanks. How are you holding up?"

"Things are pretty good, just staying busy with work. But uh, you and Cedric are getting pretty serious, huh?"

"Yeah, things have been going well. Cedric's a great guy; I really can't imagine myself with anybody else. Things just seemed to come together perfectly."

"Yeah? He's always been my best friend, but sometimes he makes decisions that aren't the best. I mean, we all have, but sometimes things really bother him."

My face displayed confusion, my eyebrows scrunched together as I grew inquisitive and asked, "What are you trying to say?"

"I'm not trying to sway you one way or another but Cedric has a temper. He can be kind of a jealous guy. You know how guys can get. Just take your time and really get to know him. Things may have changed since college."

After getting off the phone with Kendal, I was taken aback by our conversation. That was the first time he had voiced his concern. He was very direct and didn't seem to have any ill intent.

Cedric had shared bits and pieces of stories with me throughout our time together. He excitedly explained how he led the Tigers to the Division 1 Championship and the NCAA tournament. He boasted that he and Kendal joined the student counsel and got eleven thousand students to sign a petition to get the parking meters removed from campus. From what I gathered later in our relationship and the stories he shared with me, Cedric had good and some alarming relationships. There were remnants of scuffles and issues with the women he previously dated. Surprisingly, he openly admitted that he regretted some of the things that were said and done.

He enjoyed his young adult time and reaped the benefits that all-star athletes had. He was in control of his social life, academics, relationships and reputation by the results he generated on the basketball court. No one turned him down and others envied him. The early success and skill set accomplished during his role as an athlete definitely molded his personality.

Cedric and I dated for a year and a half before we married. We were both thirty years old with plenty of experiences making us ready to settle down. He and I proudly committed to being celibate until we were married. I didn't know if this created unwanted stress, but this commitment was unwavering for me.

Once, one of my friends revealed to me that she was in an abusive relationship. I was stunned because I'd met the guy and he appeared to be a great catch, but apparently, he morphed into a different person behind closed doors. I was heartbroken that she struggled with this situation alone. Likewise, I overheard my Mom and aunt talking about how aunt Cece was admitted to the hospital. She had an incident with her boyfriend one night when he was drunk.

No one openly shared these encounters or talked about these types of situations. It was discussed through whispers and then tapered off and swept under the rug. They happened and then disappeared without warning or advice.

Despite the brief rumors about what happened between Cedric and his former girlfriends, I thought of it as petty and wasn't one to entertain gossip. Cedric had been a perfect gentleman to me. I learned and understood his way of communication, which worked for the both of us. I recognized his sense of leadership on the first day he and I met and I valued that. Even though I had a strong-willed personality, I allowed him to be the man.

CHAPTER 7
ALL I CAN PROMISE IS THAT I WILL LOVE YOU

Cedric got down on his knees and proposed to me right before dinner on October 29th, 1990 at my condo. I said yes! It was a beautiful evening in downtown Minneapolis. The main front window across from my kitchenette overlooked Marquette Place. It had a gorgeous view of the sunset and peeks of the downtown skyline. It wasn't often that I'd see both, but this night was clear and picturesque. Cedric told me that he was offering me all of his love. He said he would always love me and wanted to spend the rest of his life together. For dinner, we made chicken, dressing, salad, macaroni and cheese and buttered rolls. We ate a delicious meal, talked and smiled the entire evening.

We planned to have our wedding eight months later in Minneapolis at Progressive Baptist Church. Cedric grew up Penacostal and I grew up in the Lutheran Church. I found the church when I moved to Minneapolis to begin college and attended for a year or so. My college roommate invited me to Progressive on Sunday. It was active with praise, worship and good preaching by the Reverend and his wife. Cedric didn't have a home church when I met him, so he began attending Progressive with me. We were both comfortable with the church family and enjoyed the pastor's sermons and teachings. At this point, Cedric had only spoken to my mom on the telephone. I spoke to his mom on the phone as well so I thought it was time to introduce him to my mom.

Cedric and I drove to Chicago about a week later so that he could meet my family. After meeting Cedric for the first time, I called Mom and told her that I'd met someone special and that I thought he would be my husband. She was happy for me and asked when I met him? "Just now," I said, "Just this evening at the Perimeter," I exclaimed. I could tell Mom was smiling from ear-to-ear even though she was on the other end of the telephone. I could always feel her smile.

"Baby, I'm happy for you. You haven't been this excited about meeting anyone before, so I can't wait to meet this young man."

Four weeks later, we arrived at the two-flat brick building I grew up in at about six that evening. Cedric drove for eight hours from Minneapolis to Chicago. When we exited off Hwy 290 onto Cicero Avenue, I could tell by the look on Cedric's face that he was surprised to see such a degraded neighborhood as we continued to drive south to Mom's house.

"This neighborhood has declined over the past fifteen years. All of the vacant lots and empty store front buildings used to be full of life and thriving with businesses," I explained.

Cedric commented with a light smile, "My snow bunny grew up in the hood!"

"Cedric, it didn't always use to be this way. I grew up in a very loving and safe environment; this wasn't it. It's changed because of many reasons. You do understand the problems that have plagued inner cities over the past decade, don't you?"

Cedric gave me a nod along with a big smile and said, "I can't wait to meet your Mom."

Cedric parked the Toyota pick-up truck in front of the house. The neighborhood had changed. Many of the duplex homes on the blocks in and around the area were now open lots with debris and weeds growing in spots where homes used to sit. A number of them had been abandoned or foreclosed on and then torn down. From the time I left home to attend college in 1979 until now, in 1990, the west side neighborhood had declined in presence, vibrancy and value. We got out of the truck and walked toward the house, opened the black rod iron fence and walked up the stairs to the front door. It only took Mom a few minutes to open the door after I rang the bell. She had a vibrant, beautiful smile and was full of energy. "Oh, there's my baby girl! I am so happy that you two made it safely. You must be Cedric. Brenda has told me all about you." She gave us both big hugs and we walked towards the kitchen. I put Cedric's bag in my brother's old room, which was now the guest room. Then I ventured off to place my bag in the bedroom my sister and I used to share. I knew they really wanted to meet and I could tell they both wanted to make sure the other felt their gratitude. Cedric was tall and handsome with sensual brown eyes that were entrancing. His smile and the way he carried himself made me feel good about being with him. When he held me in his broad and muscular arms, I felt safe and happy. I thought Mom would just love him.

    Cedric was really interested in learning more about the community and wanted to know if developers had approached Mom about selling her building. Cedric and Mom sat down at the kitchen table and talked about the Chicago area. Mom shared how developers had abandoned the area and begun to focus on revitalizing the downtown area by rebuilding abandoned buildings into expensive condominiums. Cedric explained the manner in which developers and contractors follow the movement of those who can invest in property. When property owners leave communities, developers follow their demands and then the developer begins to look for investments; they choose areas of demand. Unfortunately, this hurts the African American communities because what remains is a shell of progress and memories of the thriving neighborhood it used to be.

Cedric went on and on about his business, goals and opinions regarding the contracting industry. Mom listened attentively as her wide eyes studied his face. She'd release her smile while cleverly reserving her knowledge so she could learn more about him. She'd nod and just smile with her calm and warm demeanor. Her curled, black hair was pulled back neatly off her beautiful medium brown skin face. Intermittently, she'd run her hand back through her hair as she listened. Occasionally, she interjected with a comment of agreement or clarification but that was about it. Cedric spoke about his parents and how he grew up in a strict church environment. He made a point to highlight the fact that both of his brothers were ministers and pastored their own church. He didn't bite his tongue when he started talking about how he loved the Lord. I overheard Cedric say many times that he guaranteed his love for me. As I entered the room, I could see that it made Mom blush and smile even more.

"Brenda's the outspoken one in the family. I noticed that you're pretty talkative. She's the type who says what's on her mind. You two are just alike," Mom admitted cheerfully.

"Mrs. Cole, I love your daughter just the way she is. I'm excited about marrying her. Like I promised her, I love her now and I'll always love her. She's my snow bunny." Cedric reached over, grabbed my hand, pulled me toward him and affectionately kissed me on the cheek.

My mother is a loving and hardworking woman with a quiet spirit. Growing up, I rarely saw her lose her temper and she was always there to please our family including Dad, prior to his passing. Once my brother, sister and I left home to attend college and her companion moved in, she made herself available to him as well. I later found out that after they ended their fifteen-year relationship, he had been verbally abusive to my mother. She never really discussed it and I didn't bring it up either. I sensed that their relationship was strained at times, but I respected their wishes and stayed out of their business because he appeared to make her happy.

My mom was intelligent, but I think when it came to men, she lacked the confidence to confront the maladaptive use of power. Instead, she withdrew and preferred to simply remain silent or agree with what was being said. My mom went back to college at the age of forty-six and graduated with her degree when she was fifty. My mother was a fair-skinned woman with defined African American features. She never knew her Dad, so her inspection of anyone I brought home was timid and not like it would have been if she'd experienced the same with her Dad. Her disposition was always clear with her children. We did what she asked of us, simple because controversy wasn't her thing; she avoided it.

I noticed that Mom allowed Cedric to be the man and she always advised my sister and I to do the same when it came to men. She liked Cedric and told me that she thought he was a nice young man. My mom wasn't the type to disagree in a way that would cause commotion, but she always communicated what was on her mind. It was up to others, to decide what to do with the information. After my dad passed, she became both our mother and father. As long as there was order in the house and we were safe from harm, she was content.

We unpacked our things while Mom started dinner. Christian, who was all grown up now and living on his own called to say that he was stopping by for dinner to meet Cedric. He congratulated me on our engagement and said he was looking forward to finally meeting him. When Christian arrived home, he made himself comfortable as usual. He put his leather jacket on the back of the dining room chair, grabbed the remote and a tanner pillow from the sofa. He plopped down on the Chenille natural jute rug and began watching WWF wrestling on channel thirty-two. Cedric finished unpacking his things before joining Christian. They made an immediate connection.

"Hey you must be the infamous groom to be, welcome to the family, I'm Christian."

He stood up and gave Cedric a handshake and a hug. Christian was twenty-four years old and fulfilled his enlistment in the Navy. Additionally, he completed two years of college at the University of Denver, but he was still trying to find himself.

"Man, it's nice to meet you. Brenda said you're her favorite little brother."

They started laughing as I entered the living room and sat down on the rug with Christian. I grabbed his neck and pulled him toward me to get a hug and said, "Yeah, he's my favorite and only. What have you been up to? And where are you working?"

He hugged me back and replied, "Hey big sis, good to see you! You look great!" I smiled at his compliment. "I've been trying to get a job with you." He fell back onto the sofa and started laughing. "No, but seriously, I'm trying to start a band. And, I've been working out because I'm going to tryout for the WWF and see what happens." He looked great. Christian was attractive and had Dad's eyes blended with Mom's attractive features. He had a soft, milk chocolate complexion and his eyes held a deep kindness in them.

"Always follow your dreams," I told him. "So, where's your day job?"

"I work at Shinner's piano store and I'm a waiter at Bennigans," he explained cheerfully.

Growing up, I played the drums and when Christian was old enough, he began playing too. From there, he starting playing the piano and actually cultivated his talent and was able to play by ear. He did studio work and participated in numerous band activities in school.

The conversation between Cedric and Christian transitioned from Cedric talking about his love for me to Christian considering working for Cedric. He thought Christian could help him find opportunities to seek contracts in some of the developing neighborhoods in the Chicago area.

A few minutes later, Mom walked into the living room wearing her apron and a dishtowel draped across her right shoulder. Casually interrupting the conversation, she asked if we could do her a favor and go to Jewel's grocery store to get some shredded cheese. I appreciated the break because Cedric had the tendency to go overboard when speaking about his contracting business.

Cedric, Christian and I settled into the Toyota pickup truck he used for travel and his daily grind. It was a dark blue, four-wheel drive with an extended cab big enough for a ton of groceries plus three adults. We drove about fifteen minutes on Central Avenue until we arrived at Jewel's. Cedric volunteered to go inside and purchased the shredded cheese for Mom. She was preparing a turkey and noodle casserole and needed shredded, white cheese to sprinkle on top along with crushed garlic and onion croutons.

While Cedric was inside the store, Christian and I talked about old times before discussing the wedding and the preparations I needed from him. It was unusually nice out. Since Cedric left the keys in the truck, we put down the windows and felt a refreshing mild breeze. Sixty-five degrees during the second week of November was considered a beautiful and almost perfect day in Chicago. As Christian and I continued to talk about work, love and life lessons, Cedric jumped in the truck and handed me a plastic Jewel bag. He put his seatbelt on, checked the rear mirror and took off.

I sat in the passenger's seat with my black sunglasses on simply enjoying the moment. I opened the plastic Jewel bag on my lap and noticed a box of

Velveeta cream cheese, gum and a small bag of roasted almonds, which was a snack for Cedric. "Hey babe, thanks for the gum, how did you know that I was low?"

Cedric winked at me as he continued to drive. I pulled the box of cheese out of the bag, held it in my hand so that he could see it and said, "Cedric, we were supposed to get shredded cheese for Mom's casserole. What is the Velveeta cheese for?"

"She can shred the cheese with a shredder, that's the kind my Mom used. Once it's shredded, no one will know the difference. It'll still taste like cheese," Cedric replied.

"Cedric, you can't assume that. Mom specifically said to pick up shredded cheese and you bought a box of Velveeta. She wanted the kind in the zip bag, like Kraft or the Jewel brand," I stated.

"Brenda, your Mom will know what to do with that cheese, trust me. It will only take her a few minutes to slice the Velveeta into blocks and run it across a shredder. Don't make a big deal out of it. I don't see an issue here." Cedric squinted his eyes as he spoke.

"Cedric, I'm not making a big deal. I'm just asking why you would buy this type of cheese instead of what Mom asked for?" Cedric became silent instead of replying. He continued to drive focusing on the traffic ahead. "Babe, this isn't what Mom wanted. She needed the cheese to sprinkle on top of the casserole."

"Brenda! You heard me the first time. I'm not going to repeat myself. Cheese is cheese!" Cedric's volume began to increase as he motioned his right hand up and down.

"Please keep your voice down, you don't have to yell," I told him.

"I'm not yelling. If you listened to what I said, this conversation would be over. Cheese is cheese," he said, making certain to clearly enunciate his words. I could tell this argument was escalating, so I stopped talking.

I could see Christian in the back astounded by the turn of the conversation. The sound in the truck was reduced to the hum of the motor and an occasional thump as we continued to drive over familiar potholes on Central Avenue. Silence has the tendency to allow the feeling of inner awareness to gradually seep in. It was undeniable that all of us felt the thick tension in the air and we knew it was time to assess and understand why an argument over cheese developed. Cedric and I had arguments like this frequently and sometimes it caused us not to speak to one another for days. I never fully understood the real reason behind it, but I knew that life's challenges seemed to escalate our stress and create more arguments. With work, planning a wedding, trying to put closure on past relationships, managing a business and thinking about our future as husband and wife, the general stress of it all seemed paramount. Unfortunately, I remember that we never prayed during these times.

We finally made it back to Mom's. She was in the kitchen preparing dinner when Christian handed her the Jewel bag with the box of Velveeta cheese it in.

"Mom, please don't ask about the cheese. Do you have a shredder?" I asked.

"Shredder? Why would I need my shredder?"

I looked at Christian and shrugged my shoulders. I knew Mom well.

Christian shook his head and waved his hand toward the pantry, "Is it in the pantry?"

"I'm not sure," Mom replied. "Would you mind checking? I normally don't shred cheese for my casserole. I just sprinkle it on top with my crushed garlic croutons. What kind of cheese did you buy?"

Christian said, "Cedric and Brenda had a big argument because Cedric bought a box of Velveeta instead of the shredded kind. So if you could just use your shredder and not say anything, that might be best."

I cut my eyes at him and headed outside.

Mom untied her apron, dropped it on the back of the chair and called out to me, "Brenda! Brenda come here!" She followed me down the hallway and peeked into the living room. Cedric was sitting quietly on the sofa.

Mom opened the front door and saw me sitting on the banister on the front porch. "Why'd you leave the kitchen so fast to sit out here?"

"I just needed some fresh air," I answered dismissively.

"Well, dinner should be ready in about fifteen minutes. Have you and Cedric really been arguing?" She walked out onto the front porch letting the door shut softly behind her and sat next to me. "Baby, you're getting married soon and right now you don't seem so happy. Just because you have a disagreement doesn't mean you should be unhappy. Do you want to talk about it?"

"No. It's nothing really. I am happy; I just don't like when we argue. And, it's not that we argue, I think everyone does that, it's the way Cedric responds. He raises his voice and waves his arms around; he's so animated and it's completely unnecessary. I think people can have disagreements without all of that. So I'm just out here to give him some space. I think when we argue or disagree about something, the natural process of expressing it always seems to go to the extreme with him. I know he's under a lot of stress with the contracting business and he's trying to get his contracting license upgraded. But I don't have to like his means of releasing his stress. That's all there is to it."

    I got up and followed my mother inside and helped prepare the table. Cedric and I sat next to each other and ate dinner in silence. Christian commented on how good the casserole tasted. He took a bite and said, "Cheese is cheese, right Cedric?" I lunged my foot into his shin beneath the table and he broke out in laughter.

CHAPTER 8
HERE COMES THE BRIDE

I spent every extra minute I had to prepare for my wedding. Work was extremely busy so I had to use my time management skills to juggle both. My mom and sister lived in Chicago at the time, so I had to depend on my relationships and contacts in Minnesota to help me plan the logistics. My beautician at Lynette's Hair Concepts put me in touch with a friendly and successful caterer. Gladys was a middle-aged woman who had a small restaurant on the South Side of Minneapolis. It was similar to Sweetie Pies in St. Louis, Missouri but on a much smaller scale. Gladys and her sons made the best chicken wings, potato salad, collard greens, barbequed baked beans, boiled cabbage, salad, roasted brisket and red beans and rice in the state of Minnesota. She agreed to cater my wedding.

One of my co-workers scheduled an appointment for me to visit a stylist at Dayton's department store's bridal shop. I found the most unbelievable strapless, full-lace wedding gown with a matching head vail and train for a reasonable price. Cedric and I attended Progressive Baptist Church located in a quaint older established community on the southeast corner of St. Paul. They had an award-winning choir and had birthed several members of the infamous gospel group, The Sounds of Blackness. The preaching was gut-wrenching and could make you stand on your feet for at least a third of the sermon. The congregation included an assorted crowd ranging from young to old. Pastor Bell was passionate about marriage counseling. She was relentless when it came to teaching engaged couples how love becomes more complete when Christ lives in us and is put first. Her teachings focused on faith, hope and love. Her consultations guided us on fragrant loving, kindness and truth. Love is the most powerful defender.

We planned a small wedding and the crowd in the sanctuary turned around simultaneously when the back church doors opened to the tune of "Here Comes the Bride." I firmly held onto Christian's arm as he escorted me down the aisle. One hundred and fifty people watched my every move during the three minutes it took me to reach the pulpit. I was both nervous and delighted as I stood in front of my husband-to-be, exchanged our vows and took his hand in marriage. My heart was thumping with elation. The smile on my face never faded and our eyes locked as Pastor Bell spoke.

"Do you, Cedric, take Brenda to be your lawful wedded wife?"

"I do."

"And do you, Brenda, believe in and plan to fit in with your husbands plans as you submit to each other and honor Christ?"

"I do."

"I now pronounce you husband and wife. You may kiss the bride."

I heard a thunderous applause, but it sounded faint and far away as Cedric gently embraced my waist and pulled me close to him, softly comforting my lips with his. He pulled away for a brief moment. Long enough for me to feel my adrenaline surging through my body and my heart race with excitement. After I took a deep breath, gazing lovingly into his eyes, he kissed me again. This time, it was more passionate. We had lost all mindfulness that the crowd was watching attentively. We walked down three steps onto the red carpet leading to the center isle in unison.

Pastor Bell announced, "I present to you, Mr. and Mrs. Tulane!"

We made our way down the isle as guests reached out to shake our hands and rice fell from the air. Completely elated, we continued to walk hand in hand towards the double doors to exit. Wedding guests gathered outside of the church with glorious smiles and congratulatory greetings. Cedric and I took it all in as we made our way to the white town car decorated with a sign that said, "Just Married," and other paraphernalia parked right outside of the church. Christian volunteered to be the designated driver and chauffeur. Overwhelmed with joy and excitement, Christian drove us to our reception location at the Chart House on Summit Avenue in St. Paul. It was a newly renovated mansion that was converted into a magnificent bed and breakfast resort.

My brother took his time driving us to the reception. Cedric and I were all over each other, cuddling, laughing and holding hands in the back seat. The car had a beverage rack attached to the drivers side door. There were a couple bottles of champagne awaiting us. After Cedric popped a bottle, we held up our crystal glasses and toasted to loving each other forever.

When we arrived at the Chart House, most of the guests were already enjoying the live piano music. Cedric held my hand as we made our way to the wedding party dining area. There were twelve of us which included Cedric's best friend, Mike, who was the best man, my sister as the maid of honor, four groomsmen and bridesmaids.

The Chart House was a unique Victorian mansion that was renovated and converted into a bed and breakfast resort. Guests stayed upstairs in the lofts and many just hung out and relaxed in the massive leather chairs in the executive library den. The first floor of the Chart House had an open format. The antique dining area was in the center with the piano room and entertainment area on one side and nook for lounging and meeting on the opposite side. There was a large screened in sun porch in the back, which had a view of the pedal pond and forest. The room looked simply elegant. Cedric and I, along with the rest of the wedding party, sat in the center of the room. People cheered and congratulated us and then they'd wander off to indulge in the delectable buffet. We ate, joked, laughed and enjoyed our beautiful time of matrimony.

Mike, Cedric's best man, gave a speech about commitment, loyalty and love. He shared his account of how Cedric and I blossomed into lovebirds. The reception was beautiful. Cedric would not leave my side. He was very attentive and affectionate throughout the evening.

As the crowd began to disperse, Teri approached us and asked Cedric for his assistance.

"Cedric, I know you want to stay with Brenda because she's your new bride and all, but I'm struggling with all of the gifts you guys received. I want to put them upstairs in the loft so they're out of the way when the servers begin cleaning. Or would you prefer they go in the trunk of the car?"

"I think we should put them in the car. I'll help you," Cedric told Teri. He flashed a beautiful smile at me before he turned back and followed Teri.

While Cedric and Teri were preoccupied, Mike walked up to me and said, "Your husband isn't going to like this, but I'm stealing the bride."

Mike literally scooped me up almost as if he were going to carry me across the threshold. Instead, he slipped me through back door and into his black Mercedes. Two of the groomsmen were in the back seat and the others were in the car behind us.

"Brenda, stealing the bride is a tradition. I didn't want to say anything inside because I couldn't get Cedric away from you. We're taking you to the Yongers Club. Teri did a good job distracting Cedric. And don't worry, she and the girls will bring him over in a little bit."

"I think this is a fun idea and all and I know stealing the bride is a tradition, but did you guys check with Cedric before doing this?"

The guys in the backseat were laughing. They were loud and teasing me about having to cater to Cedric now that we are married.

Romar boldly announced from the backseat, "I know one day I'll find a woman like you. I had my eye on Karen all day; she's single right? I know she'll be at Yongers in a minute and I think I'm going to make my move."

John nudged Romar in the arm and asked, "What moves do you have? Oh, hello baby, my name is

Romar. That's not strong or smooth enough for a lady like Karen. You've got to come strong if you want to get the attention of a perfectly classy woman like her."

I listened to these grown men joke and take light jabs at each other. It was funny and great to see them having a good time. As I listened to the conversation, I thought about Karen who was one of my dear college friends. I didn't hesitate to ask her to be a bridesmaid.

I always felt like Cedric had some sort of suspicions about Karen. We went to college together and became adults in the fast life of Minneapolis and made mistakes like everyone else. When Cedric found the cancelled check for twenty-five hundred dollars in my Lipstick Allí box that I'd written out to Karen, he seemed to wonder about what type of relationship we truly had. He didn't go out of his way to pry since that happened in the past, but I still sensed Cedric was jealous of our relationship. Because he didn't discuss it, I think there was a perception that we had some sort of secret.

Karen was private and sophisticated. We did have a secret, but it wasn't one to be proud of. Out of respect for one another, we just kept it to ourselves. I gave the money to Karen to invest but the deal went bad. She paid me back but I kept the cancelled check to remind me of my stupidity. Karen's boyfriend was a drug dealer and he took the money from her and invested it in some sort of scheme. When he got caught, somehow the money disappeared. At the time, Karen was a realtor and that money was supposed to be used to invest in a duplex. I gave it to her as a down payment on rental property. We made amends and when she fulfilled her obligation to return the money, I let it go.

Mike parked right in front of Yongers. They knew we were arriving because the valet immediately took care of both cars. Mike handed the valet his keys, we went inside to a cheering crowd and pulsating dance music. I smiled and laughed beyond control as I entered and saw many of our guests greeting me with more love and congratulatory words. They had planned this after all. I didn't think twice about whether or not Cedric was aware of what was going on any longer. This really was a nice surprise and the celebration continued. I made my way to the dance floor with the groomsmen crew.

Teri and Cedric finished placing the wedding gifts in the trunk of the car. Christian jumped in the driver's seat and was ready for what happened next. The Chart House wasn't empty yet because many of the guests still lingered to nibble on wedding cake and what was left of the buffet. Teri noticed that Cedric had been pacing the floor in the main hallway leading to the piano room.

"What's wrong Cedric, did you lose something?" Cedric looked uncomfortable and began to loosen his bow tie.

"Yeah, my wife!" he snapped.

Teri smiled and told him, "She's not lost, trust me. I can't really say anything, but I want you to come with me, there's a surprise for you."

Cedric began pacing the floor and said, "I'm not going anywhere until I find Brenda. Brenda! Brenda! Babe, where are you?" he yelled.

"Cedric, please don't yell. Your guests are still here and there's no need to yell. Brenda stepped out, she's not here. It's part of the surprise."

"Surprise? I don't want to be surprised! What in the hell happened to my wife? Where is she? Brenda!"

Cedric began walking through the Chart House searching and shouting.

"Sshhh, Cedric, let's go. I'll take you to her. Please just calm down. Let's go."

She caught up with him and grabbed his arm as he approached the stairs to the loft area. Cedric pulled away and continued to walk upstairs, speaking loudly, "Are you up here? Where are you?" Five minutes later, Teri watched Cedric walk down the stairs looking defeated. She grabbed his hand and took him outside and walked him toward the car.

"Brenda's at Yongers Club with Mike, Romar, Tyler, John, Curtis and the rest of the guest. It's a tradition to steal the bride. This was supposed to be a fun idea, not a trick and not a ploy to upset you. We were just trying to have fun and surprise you."

Teri motioned Cedric to get in the backseat.

Christian said, "I guess you're ready for Yongers. I hope you'll be surprised, man." Christian wasn't aware of what just happened. "Do you really know what the significance of stealing a bride is all about?"

"No," Cedric said. "Why don't you tell me what it's all about?"

"Hundreds of years ago it was customary for a best man to accompany an eligible bachelor to find the woman of his choice. This was common in communities where good women were in short supply. The purpose of selecting a best man was to pick someone who could strong arm anyone, as the future bridegroom captured a woman from a neighboring community when there weren't any available ones in his own community. So, the best man's job wasn't always to just guard the ring. Another custom is that the best man remained at the side of the groom along with his new wife.

"Mike is a snake, I'm going to get him," Cedric snarled. "Thanks for the history lesson."

"Cedric, please just act surprised and please don't show out. Never let anyone see you sweat," Christian said smoothly.

Christian and Teri laughed and then looked at Cedric in a playful manner. Cedric was calm; he joined in and laughed it off.

When Cedric, Christian and Teri entered Yongers, the crowd cheered louder as the groom found his bride and joined her on the dance floor.

CHAPTER 9
BUILDING OUR DREAM

We had been in our new house for approximately two years. The house was built by one of the most desirable builders in the Twin Cities area. Cedric oversaw the entire project. He was there when the surveyors broke ground. He monitored the process when the builders laid the foundation. Cedric was instrumental in picking out the smallest details such as lighting fixtures. He recommended we upgrade the wiring and plumbing so the inner foundation would be solid. He didn't want us to worry about faulty wiring or leaks later. Although Cedric's specialty was building home gazebos and decks, he was very knowledgeable about houses. I learned so much about buying and building a home from him.

A few years before buying our new house, Cedric and I would walk through this particular development and marvel at how big and beautiful the homes were and how sophisticated the community presence was. Seeing all of the homes being built from the ground up was exhilarating and motivating to us. We both felt right at home when we strolled through the neighborhood. The homeowners were diverse, professional, middle-class families. We worked tirelessly, sacrificed and planned for the upgrade. We used to tell each other "We are moving on up to The Big House." Deep down, we both knew that was the community and neighborhood we belonged in. Principals, bankers, doctors and contractors lived in this particular development.

When we finally closed on this property, next to getting married and having our beautiful daughter, Nia, it was the proudest thing we'd accomplished. The homes were selling fast and we were able to qualify for one of the last homes being built. The investment we made in our first house paid off because we increased the value of that home by ninety thousand dollars. We used the equity in that home to make a healthy down payment on what we called, The Big House.

Our first house was a mid-sized two-story starter home with an unfinished basement and a big backyard with a lawn that needed major work. We lived there for five years. It was our first house that we bought it together. Cedric was familiar with building codes and home specifications so he put a plan together to finish our basement. Nia's fourth birthday party was held in our partially finished basement but casually made its way throughout the house.

Not long after, we decided to finish the basement ourselves. He measured the exposed walls so that he could install sheet rock. Cedric designed the blueprint for the extra bathroom we built. After spreading grout and laying a hundred and twenty pieces of ceramic tile, I never wanted to get on my knees again. We installed an eight-foot Koehler tub and a matching vessel sink. The bathroom was a nice addition to the lower level. As though that wasn't enough, we pulled up the entire backyard. It was filled with bad grass, mostly weeds and crabgrass. Cedric rented a lawn cutter, which sliced about an inch of grass in 3" x 5" cubes. On one Mother's Day after church, we spent the entire afternoon outside pulling up old dirt and grass. Cedric rolled the four-blade grass cutter and I moved the 3" x 5" slab of old grass to the side and rolled it up and stacked it. Cedric rolled the grass cutter on a section of the yard. I pushed another sliced piece aside, rolled it and stacked it. This continued until about 8:00 in the evening until the entire backyard was bare and we could only see brown dirt, which was all that was underneath the weeds and crabgrass. I learned so much about home expansion and how to increase the value of property form that experience.

Cedric was a good teacher. The things he taught me saved thousands of dollars. I'm grateful to have learned this from Cedric because he was a good teacher. The upgrades that Cedric completed on our first house increased the value by ninety thousand dollars. We were proud of the accomplishments that we made together.

The cedar wood sun porch Cedric helped build seemed to impress everyone who visited. The wood was freshly cut and mounted piece by piece lending the feel of a cabin. The custom-made black, exposed steel stove sat on a concrete slab in the corner of the room. It felt comfortable and cozy. It was our favorite room in the house.

One year, after we completed the upgrades, we listed the house to sell ourselves. I had a great time showing the house and convincing several house hunters to put our house on the top of their must purchase list. Eventually, we sold our beautiful starter home. It was a bittersweet moment. We invested so much of ourselves into this house, but the housing market was booming and we had an opportunity to upgrade and build our first home.

This one was going to be the home we would retire in. I just knew it.

We scheduled our property closings on the same day so that we could move into our newly built home only three miles away. After moving most of our belongings into the new house, we went back for one final check and decided to have our last meal there. Cedric, Nia and I ordered a pizza and sat on the floor of the cedar sunroom. We ate while reminiscing about our neighbors and joked about how we'd miss their odd ways.

I talked to one of the neighbors a few times throughout the week. She was a homemaker, but I think she had an undying yearning to be someplace besides home. Cedric and I would see her occasionally at a few of the jazz clubs we went to. Intuitively, I knew she wasn't happy. What disturbed me the most was all of the hollering and screaming that steadily streamed out of their house. Cedric and I had numerous arguments, but I'm certain the neighborhoods were not privy to them. We were both headstrong and made our points on various topics we discussed, but we were not loud people. Unfortunately, our neighbors had that dreadful reputation. Their arguments came down in a trickle, but eagerly transitioned into a downpour. Although Carol seemed unhappy, she never really opened up or asked for help. Instead, she'd compliment me on how my family seemed perfect and how we appeared to get along and enjoy one another. We did look that way, but it wasn't always our reality. We invested so much in the exterior of our lives that the interior still needed work. People only saw what we wanted them to see.

Somehow, I managed to get a pit in my stomach when I'd hear her husband's diminutive profanity fly out of his mouth when he yelled at her. I couldn't stand it, let alone imagine any man talking to a woman and especially a child that way. We could hear it so I imagined others could too. Sometimes it went on for hours and others, it lasted for a short while. The homes on our street were about ten feet apart making it easy to take in the neighbors' personal business. I noticed when Carol walked out of her house wearing sunglasses; she never approached me or glanced my way. Deep down, I understood why she didn't have anything to say because I knew the feeling.

Cedric and I argued about insignificant things. He was under pressure at work and had some issues with child support or a maternity suit that mysteriously dropped in his lap by someone he dated before I met him. While he never discussed it with me or acknowledged this child, I knew this was a turning point for him. With all of this boiling inside of him, our arguments had the tendency to escalate without warning. Often, they developed over the most trivial topics. I was sitting at the kitchen table when he grabbed my face. His right thumb was pressing forcefully right on top of my right cheekbone directly beneath my eye. The rest of his hand straddled the other side of my face. His grip was strong and caused me to stand. I grabbed his wrist and screamed, "Let me go! Let me go, before I call the police!" He let go, simply left the kitchen and disappeared upstairs.

We were expecting guests for dinner and Cedric planned on making lasagna. Our guests were on their way and I couldn't think of any other way of handling the situation than to quickly pull my composure together. I went into the bathroom and looked in the mirror. I didn't know how this rapidly became such a normal part of my life. My cheeks were a little flushed, although the lower part of my right eye was tingling. I knew I'd have a black eye.

Suddenly I thought of how my own life must relate to Carol's. I cringed inside as I pulled a tissue out of the box and dabbed the tears falling from my eyes. The tissue underneath and around the eyelid was fragile and bruised easily with the slightest blunt force. A fracture of the soft bones or the pressure around the delicate eye area can trap the soft tissues and cause engorged blood vessels, thus darkening color underneath the eye. Much like Carol, I didn't approach anyone when I left the house with sunglasses on either. I was determined to leave these memories behind. However, I wasn't at the point where I felt trapped because there were a lot of good things about my marriage, I thought the bad things were worth suppressing. I wanted it to work. I let go of the few incidents that occurred and viewed them as stress induced situations. In reality, it was denial.

I was determined to start over and enjoy a different lifestyle in our new home. Cedric was so proud of our accomplishments; he walked with his chest out and had a renewed resilience and determination about him.

One evening in late November, there was a tragic incident that brought us on our knees in prayer and reflection. I received a call from Cedric on a Saturday evening around eight. It was dark outside, but the sky was clear. Highway 12 wasn't illuminated enough and during that time of the year it always seemed to be a bit obscure. Cedric was driving back from a project and stopped at our rental property to measure the floors for the new carpet we needed to install. We hadn't sold the condominium I lived in prior to marrying, so we completed the upgrades ourselves and rented it. Eventually, it sold but while it was rented, the property was an excellent tax shelter. Cedric called me on that particular evening and said he was on the side of the road. He called the police because he thought he hit a deer or something. By the time the police arrived, they discovered that it wasn't a deer, but a teenage girl. Cedric was about ten miles away from home. Fortunately, I was able to get ahold of the neighbor. I asked her to babysit Nia so I could drive to the scene to be with Cedric. By the time I arrived, she had passed. The police had determined it was an accident. Witnesses told police a teenage girl was standing in median before she darted in front of his truck on one of the busiest streets in the area. He was driving the legal speed limit of forty-five mph and police found no substances were involved.

My nerves were shot and devastation sank comfortably inside of me. I couldn't believe that my husband was somewhat responsible for a human being's death. Furthermore, I could only imagine the darkness weighing down his spirit. All I could do was pray.

On occasion, Cedric would stop and have a beer after working at a contracting site or after fixing something at our rental property. On this particular night, he didn't. He wasn't ticketed nor was he taken to the police station. What happened was heartbreaking and tragic. It was beyond my comprehension as to how her family must have felt. We didn't know if she left anyone behind. My body was occupied with shock and coupled with an indescribable feeling of horror. Tears streamed heavily down my perspiring face and I could see that Cedric was in the same mental state. I couldn't breathe because I was certain this unfortunate occurrence completely devastated my husband. His disposition was quite grave in a way I'd never seen before. For a man that appeared to have so much control over his life, we were unmistakably reminded that control is nothing but an illusion. None of us truly have it. It was taken from him in a very dark and unexpected moment. When his illusion was stripped from him, it was taken from me too, because he was my husband and what hurt him, shot to my core. That awful night continued and it felt as though it went on for the longest time. All we could do was pray.

We all have situations, which are simply beyond our control or things that cannot be foreseen. However, devastation has the ability to take shape in all of us for better or worse. It has the ability to take us closer to God or deeply inward towards ourselves.

I watched this devastate Cedric and I saw in him, a lack of comprehension for what had befallen. Neither of us could imagine the pain that it caused the young girls family, nor did we know why she chose that path, but she did. We have to teach people that there are other solutions to ending pain or to stop whatever is causing us to hurt. I wondered if the young girl kept everything inside bundled up so tightly, that no one knew it was ever there. Then, I wondered if she had told someone, and if so, did anyone show her that they cared.

At this point, Cedric and I had been married for ten years. In terms of our relationship, things were good with us. We still argued about different things and both of us had strong personalities, which caused situations to escalate rather than to descend faster. There weren't any abusive incidents for several years. Past altercations remained in my mind, but they were tucked far away and were not something I thought about anymore.

Work was busy and required my time even when I was at home on my computer a lot and I traveled when necessary. I spent a great deal of time on the phone.

On many occasions, Cedric would come into the office den reciting the standard, "I see you're working again. You hardly ever spend time with Nia and I. Why don't you come and play Jenga with us?"

I'd inhale deeply before releasing a heavy breath of air and reply, "Cedric, I have to finish this report. Give me thirty minutes," I'd tell him but I knew it was increasingly difficult to pull me away from my work. There was something in my work that defined me and I found it to be a reprieve. From what, I never really specified, but it was.

My workload was always heavy. I made it a point to sneak as many kisses to Nia whenever I worked in my home office. Our way of communicating the unconditional bond of love we shared was to gently rub noses together. It led to the cutest giggles from my baby girl and her eyes were filled with a luminosity I wanted to see forever. Every hour of my work was worth it to make sure that I contributed to making her life as comfortable as I possibly could. I was certain she wouldn't understand that aspect of life, but it was necessary. I knew her father wanted more for her, but so did I.

Cedric worked evenings and weekends. I worked days so I took care of Nia before and after school. Most of the time, she was with me on weekends. When we had time together at home, predominantly on Cedric's days off, we'd go out to dinner, watch movies, attend Nia's soccer games or would grill ribs, chicken, burgers and hotdogs while enjoying the sunshine. Sometimes our time went to doing our own thing.

Although it was my fortieth birthday, it was merely another typical workday for me. Pharmaceutical sales kept me reading, learning and diving into a constant pool of evolution. I always had a plethora of things to do and I didn't leave any loose ends that day either. Cedric said he wanted to meet for cocktails right after work. We went to The Roadhouse, which was a casual restaurant and lounge in an upscale section of St. Paul, Minnesota. While Cedric and I were having cocktails, my cell phone rang. I reached inside my purse to pull it out and was surprised at the phone number on the caller ID. It was my home number. I turned to Cedric and asked, "Who's calling from the house?" He pulled his shoulders back and responded as if he had no idea. I answered, "Hello?"

My friend Linda replied, "Hey, what time will you be headed to your house?"

"Hey Linda, you're calling from my home phone. Why are you at my house?" She didn't respond; instead, I heard a click. I glanced over at Cedric inquisitively. "Is there something going on at the house?"

He swallowed the last sip of his cocktail and then with a clever grin replied, "Let's go see."

Cedric drove his truck and I jumped into my company car to follow him home. As we drove down our street, the first thing I looked for were cars parked in front of the house. I suspected a party or gathering of some sort after receiving that strange call from Linda. However, upon pulling into our driveway, I didn't see any additional vehicles anywhere in the vicinity of our house. Apparently I was wrong. When we pulled into the driveway, Cedric rolled down his window and said he was going to leave the truck in the driveway because he had to run an errand later. He had a straight face and appeared as if everything was normal. I think after suspecting something, I anticipated a little surprise after Linda's call, but it didn't look as though there was going to be one. Regardless, it didn't make sense. I parked in the garage, got out of the car and waited for Cedric in the garage. He grabbed my hand and said, "Happy Birthday baby." We walked toward the door to enter the house. I pressed the garage door remote on the wall next to the mudroom door and the garage door closed. I routinely took off my shoes, put my keys and purse on the utility counter before heading upstairs to the bedroom. I wanted to change out of my clothes, spend time with my family and relax. I smelled dinner and noticed the crock-pot and a roasting pan covered with aluminum foil sitting on the stove. As I headed upstairs, I felt a little disappointed because I thought Cedric had planned some sort of surprised gathering for me. The call from Linda was perplexing and I couldn't let it go. By the time I reached the upstairs hallway, I noticed our bedroom door was closed. We typically didn't shut our door. I opened the door and as soon as I stepped into the bedroom, the lights came on and a loud roar of people shouted in unison, "Surprise! Happy Birthday!" There were balloons, streamers and presents all over the room.

That was the most beautiful and memorable event in our dream home. Cedric and Nia went through great lengths to keep the party a secret. At this point, our marriage had been a roller coaster ride filled with highs and lows as well as surprises, but I didn't expect anything like this. We were married for seven years and I didn't expect anything like this. Cedric managed to find my planner and made a list of my closest friends to invite. Cedric contacted one of my colleagues from work to ensure I wasn't traveling for meetings during that weekend. Cedric and Nia picked out a cake. He knew I'd enjoy whatever Nia wanted so it was a two-layered white cake with chocolate icing and multi-colored sprinkles on the top that read, "Happy 40th Birthday Mom!"

Cedric prepared jambalaya with sausage, chicken and rice, grilled chicken wings, potato salad, roasted turkey in crescent rolls, a veggie tray with homemade spinach dip and punch. It was Friday, December 20, 2000 and it was beautiful.

This was the biggest surprise ever. There was a park a block away from our house. Cedric asked everyone to park there and plan to arrive between five and six that evening. He picked them up as they arrived and brought everyone to the house so I wouldn't notice all the cars. He told anyone who couldn't make it on time to come after seven. This way, I'd already be home and surprised.

Friends and colleagues rang our doorbell throughout the evening to wish me a happy birthday. We had a nice gathering of people. We danced, told jokes, engaged in robust discussions about almost everything and enjoyed great food.

As the party tapered off and eventually ended, the party was a success. I was now forty and eagerly awaiting my future. Everything seemed to be perfect. Our house was becoming more like a home and things seemed to be settling just the way I had hoped. I thought the tension that often flirted between us was going to leave us in peace. That night faded to black.

As the year 2000 drew to an end, we settled into our routine. At forty years old, I had been married for ten years. This was it. We had transitioned through some difficult times and managed to stay true to our vows, "Until death do us part." Love is patient and kind, never jealous, envious, boastful or proud. Love isn't selfish or rude and it doesn't demand its own way. It's not irritable or touchy nor does it hold grudges. Love will hardly notice when others do it wrong. It is never pleased with injustice, but rejoices when truth wins out. If you love someone, you will be loyal to that person. You will always believe in them even when they have moments they may not believe.At this time, the greatest thing I held onto was hope. I wanted my marriage to sustain and I worked diligently to release the thoughts of our past problems inclusive of abuse and uncertainty. As the pressure of maintaining our house increased, just like any other couple, we had to deal with the stress of managing expenses, working overtime, paying past due taxes, saving and plan for the future, eliminating debt and coming to grips with the fact that we still had issues with child support and a maternity suit that wasn't acknowledged. For some reason, Cedric didn't have closure with a relationship he had prior to ours. A child was born as a result of that relationship.

The purpose of fatherhood is to be involved in your child's upbringing so they have a strong guide to help them develop. Building a strong and fortified family in a healthy environment is key. I believe the father is supposed to be the leader and lover of his home as much as the provider for the spiritual and domestic needs of his family. The lingering maternity suit Cedric never wanted to discuss was his first opportunity to embrace fatherhood.

Over time, there were a few things that began to return to my thoughts. By January 2001, I was questioning our future. It was an icy weekend in January and I was rushing around cleaning the house that morning. I was planning to attend a dinner with the girls, which left me a lot of things to accomplish before then. One of my close friends was in town from Michigan and we planned to get together for old time sake. I wanted to introduce her to another friend of mine. Things took a negative turn causing Cedric and I to get into an argument about my evening plans while Nia watched. I realized that this wasn't what I wanted for my life but more importantly, my daughter. I didn't want her to think this was normal because it wasn't. Most of the time I tried to diffuse situations before they escalated but I was at the mercy of Cedric's emotional state.

Ultimately, it was up to him to let things go. I was feeling the unsettling discomfort once again and I didn't want to tip around my life nor his. I was terrified at what my beautiful little girl would think and learn. Something had to change and I was certain it would have to be me. I didn't know how but in order to do that, I'd have to change my mindset.

CHAPTER 10
I NEVER IMAGINED

It didn't take long before we were standing in front of a judge listening to him recite the facts stated on the paperwork in front of him. I never imagined we'd arrive at this point in our marriage. But it didn't matter what I thought because evidently we were there. It was disheartening for many reasons and indicated that we were nearing the end of it.

The judge stated, "In the capacity I have reviewed the police report of officers Steve and Hugh and believe the following facts to be true–"

As he began with his synopsis and ruling, I sat in my seat embarrassed and afraid by what it all meant. I could barely glance over at Cedric. It was hard enough to be in that situation with not only the man I loved but was married to. What happened to our vows? What happened to us? How was this going to affect Nia? As the judge continued, my palms grew sweaty. Love wouldn't put anyone in this position. I had a lot to figure out.

The only voice in the courtroom was the judge, and my recollection followed his every word.

"As officer Steve approached the defendant, the defendant was checking his mailbox. Officer Steve spoke with the defendant and the defendant stated that he and his wife got into a heated argument. He lashed out and she lashed back. He stated that his wife was vacuuming upstairs and continued to hit the trim on the wall. He went upstairs and asked her to stop. He stated he put his hand on her shoulder and pushed her down so that she could see where the dent was on the wall and pointed it out. He stated she got off balance and started to freak out. He then dialed 911, spoke to the dispatcher and asked for the police to come out to their house. He stated several times he was the one who called the police. Officer Steve spoke with the victim. She stated that she was in fear of physical harm as a result of the incident. She stated the defendant put his arm around her and pushed her down to make her look at the dent. She claimed he shoved her after he pointed out the dent. She stated that approximately seven or eight years ago, there was a similar incident where the defendant had struck her in the face causing it to swell. She stated she went to the hospital because she was pregnant and the defendant had been sitting on her stomach. When the defendant let go of her she ran downstairs, went into a room and shut the door. She stated she was holding the door shut with her foot and trying to dial 911–"

This was such a trivial situation to have escalated but it evolved due to Cedric's actions, our history and the fear he instilled into me. This situation wasn't the problem. It was indicative of the real problems in our marriage that were simmering beneath this unnecessary display of anger or emotional backlash.

"The defendant was placed under arrest and transported to the Minneapolis Police Department. The defendant provided a taped statement and was then transported the Hennepin County Jail," the judged stated firmly. This seemed like the beginning to the end but it wasn't; the first time was. We were standing in front of the judge because I refused to see it and do something about it then. It doesn't get better.

CHAPTER 11
THE PREVALENCE OF DOMESTIC VIOLENCE

This incident brought back dreadful memories of what happen while I was pregnant with Nia. I didn't invest in doing anything to spiritually or emotionally heal because I was too busy trying to suppress it so I could continue the marriage and pretend the dream was still available. I casually swept it under my emotional rug to hide the shame and pain. Regardless of the degree of domestic violence, I consider the first time to be the worst because it signifies what is to come if you don't do anything about it or take measures to stop it. I didn't know when or where something would happen but I knew it was in him to do so. I placed myself in a category of fear since I let it go. I softened my approach in communicating and was careful not to instigate an argument so I wouldn't upset my husband. I allowed the changes in our marriage to occurred once I accepted the first incident.

I remember that a few weeks after my stent at the hospital, the healing on the outside was apparent but it wasn't so complete on the inside. My two black eyes indicated that the skin tissue from all of the trauma and swelling was healing properly. I was embarrassed that my physical appearance let people know that I too, was *living in the black*.

It was only a week after my stay in the hospital when Cedric asked if I would go for a ride with him. He wanted to show me a special place where we could sit, relax and watch the planes transcend. He said that I'd enjoy it and that he thought it would provide some quality time for us to bond and talk outside of the business and routine in our house. We stopped and got my favorite Häagen-Dazs ice cream. French vanilla almond was my vice. I could easily devour a whole quart, especially since I was seven months pregnant. I enjoyed my ice cream while Cedric drove to an unfamiliar location. We were headed toward the airport on I-35W. Instead of exiting onto to airport campus, we took the frontage road to a canal that looked as if it sat beneath the interstate. I wasn't sure how Cedric discovered the unique viewing spot, but it was fantastic. We could see the current from the base of the canal. The water stream was strong, steady and flowed smoothly down the narrow, concrete tubular flooring. This particular canal was used for irrigation and was massive and commercialized like the ones that are built for boats.

"Mike told me about this canal. It wasn't developed to its fullest capacity because the airport renovations required use of part of the land down here. Most of it was preserved but as you can see, the airport runway is only about a mile away." He pointed east as if he could see the runway ahead. "Mike and I came here last week and just talked. So I thought I'd bring you here so we could talk and share whatever is on our mind." He smiled, leaned over and kissed me on the cheek as we sat in the car. He was waiting for me to respond.

I could tell Cedric was remorseful for what happened. However, what bothered me most was that he looked at me every day after the incident, saw my swollen face and black eyes but treated me as if I looked normal. He knew my spirit was broken when he came home and made dinner while talking about his day as if nothing had ever happened.

Interrupting my thoughts, Cedric leaned over and kissed me on the cheek as he'd done many times before. He pointed at the aircrafts as they flew into range but he didn't have my attention because my mind was elsewhere. Cedric wasn't aware that a few days prior, I visited the local police department to fill out an application to carry a gun. What irritated me after the incident was that I felt alone and completely vulnerable. I thought about protecting myself and lost faith in my husband being willing to do so. At the firearms verification department, I completed the application and placed it in the processing basket on the left side of the counter. Apparently it's normal for a man to request a firearm but the receptionist along with a few of the patrons looked at me as though I were doing something wrong. Sure, perhaps it had something to do with the fact that I was seven months pregnant and generously showing my baby bump. However, they didn't know what brought me to that place just the same as others.

After I walked through the corridor, up the narrow and partially lit stairway, I exited through the side door. I clicked my automatic keypad and faintly heard the beep indicating that my door was unlocked. I got in and stared out the window. I was sure that once the form was processed, it would be approved and I would be able to buy a gun.

It was rather easy to apply for a gun permit. My mindset had deteriorated to a rather frail state and I needed something to help get my confidence back up.

I deemed that feeling safe would do that. I thought it was a chance to improve my chances of fighting back and defend myself. I walked through the corridor, and thought about what I'd done. I was never supportive of Cedric having a gun in the house but I bought him a custom hunting rifle for his birthday a few years back. Then he sold it to help fund his bonding license and certificate. Now I was fighting violence with the ability to create more. Ultimately, Cedric sold my gift rendering me quite disappointed at first but after things became more and more tense around the house, I was relieved. I was paranoid about having a gun accessible and that close to me. Cedric's warm hand touched my arm bringing my attention back.

"Snap out of it honey. Here comes a plane. It's about to land; watch it glide."

I wasn't capable of letting go of the violence that had just transpired and stare into the sky to watch planes land. I didn't know if he was trying to divert my attention away from the situation but it wasn't possible for me to let go as long as the bruises were still visible and my spirit was broken. His touch was no longer the loving touch I used to crave. It wasn't the same and I didn't know if it would come back. Although I truly loved him, I didn't deserve this.

In a dry tone I said, "That's amazing Cedric. A plane is a perfectly engineered piece of machinery." He began to talk about how this spot was relaxing and how he wanted to bring me here to talk and spend some time opening up to each other about anything on our minds. He tried to explain how much he loved me and I was all that he had. He said he was excited that the baby would be here in a couple months but it didn't feel right because his actions could have harmed her.

My friend, Jacque, was planning my baby shower for couples. Cedric said he wanted to participate and help out.

"Have you thought about names for the baby?" he asked. I didn't respond, my thoughts had coasted away from what he was saying and I preferred to be with them. I could only think that this was far from over and although I hoped it wouldn't happen again, in my gut, I was certain it would. I was apprehensive about our future. I didn't want our child to be born into an abusive cycle. I didn't want this to ever touch her, let alone scar her.

Fear has a way of causing people to do things they ordinarily wouldn't think of. It was out of fear and coupled with desperation that I applied for a gun. I was drained from Cedric's out-of-control arguments. I told him once, "If you ever put your hands on me again, I'll kill you." At the time, I wanted him to feel the same degree of fear that he put into me. I didn't have it in me to do so, but I needed to find a way to let him know that I wasn't going to live in fear of him, although I already was. I wondered what would have happened if there was a gun in the house then.

I knew I wasn't going to tolerate domestic violence again. I couldn't. People are human and certainly subject to being upset or disappointed by something, but abuse is never the solution. It's a cowardly way to release what you can't handle. I wasn't going to raise our daughter in that type of environment and it caused me to question why I married Cedric.

I started the car and just stared lifelessly out the window trying to determine where I'd hide it. I knew I wanted a small automatic of some sort. One that was easy to use and that, of course, had a safety lock on it. I'd keep it ready in case I needed it. I loved Cedric for his brilliance and for the love he showed me, but his anger and abusive episodes were inexcusable. I wondered if I should just leave and get divorced instead of buying a gun. Somewhere inside me, I wasn't ready to give up on our marriage and divide our family. When it was good, it was good. I sounded like I was making excuses. I tried to find a solution for our marriage by buying a gun to protect myself, which didn't seem quite logical. I just didn't know what else to do.

I could count the domestic incidences between Cedric and I on hand. The worst landed me in the emergence room when I was pregnant. We'd grown together from the bottom up and supported each other so well I didn't understand it. After the first abusive incidence, there weren't anymore for a few years and then, it started up again. Initially, I thought that the first situation was a release of his stress and anger but it was all in the past. But after the second incident, I realized a pattern was developing.

I learned through my work with Women Taking Risks that the social acceptability of domestic violence differs around the world. However, in many countries, including the U.S., women between the ages of fifteen and forty-nine typically justify a husband beating his wife. Abuse is the tension-building phase to something far worse.

I leaned forward to turn up the news, I listened to them report on a young man who shot his girlfriend and then committed suicide. They stated that the couple had many domestic violence problems and no one acknowledged it or offered help. As I listened to the story, I realized that having a gun would only exacerbate the situation. A gun will escalate arguments because you know it's there to warn or protect. Nothing good can come from it. Listening to the story unfold on the radio stopped me from going home. I was heart stricken and knew that my principle of not being around guns was the right thing to do. People can say things and even bad scenario's can be pre-meditated, but if they don't have the tools to act on those thoughts, especially when they are deadly, life is preserved. I turned the radio off, removed the key from the ignition and got out of the car. I locked my door and went back into the police station. I walked down the stairs, back through the corridor and approached the registration desk. There was a fairly long line now, which I thought was interesting. Americans enjoy their freedom, especially the right to bear arms. I was surprised to see a very beautiful and professional looking, middle-aged female two spots ahead of me. I noticed that she was pregnant too and I wondered if she was in a similar situation. When I approached the counter, I asked the office to retrieve my application. I told him that I changed my mind and decided that I did not want the application processed. The name on his shirt read, Kenneth. Kenneth grabbed the stack of applications from a wire basket and asked me for my last name. He quickly found my application and handed it to me. As I headed towards the exit, I tore the application into little pieces, tossed it in the trash and left. I felt relieved. Although I was afraid of

Cedric's anger returning at some point, I decided that a gun wasn't the answer to my situation.

I thought about my aunt and how she kept a gun beneath her bed. She'd grab it and wave it around quite liberally when someone undesirable approached her house. When I was young, I remember visiting my Aunt CeCe. She was sitting in the window with a black forty-five pistol on her lap. I overheard my parents talking about my aunt's forward attitude, but actually seeing her with her gun surprised me because I'd never seen a gun up close. It didn't look dangerous at all. In fact, it looked like a toy. But the neighborhood she lived in was infested with crime, so I guess that was her way of keeping herself safe.

My mind slowly faded to black when Cedric tapped me on my hand and gently raised it to his mouth and kissed it.

"Babe, you seem preoccupied with something. Are you watching the planes land? Did you see the last one?" He slowly lifted my dark sunglasses and kissed me on my upper left cheek causing me to flinch. He carefully placed his thumb on the black and blue circle underneath my eye and looked at me with such grief and said, "I'm so sorry Brenda. You're still beautiful to me. This will never happen again. I promise, I'm sorry."

I thought about our marriage and the violence that had occurred. I realized that having a weapon of any sort would only aggravate the situation. Once my adrenaline escalated, the probability that the gun would be introduced to the situation was high. I didn't love the violence, but I did love Cedric. Perhaps I needed to love him from a distance.

Nothing would be worth a devastating end. I thought of the precious life of the young girl again and it pained me deeply. If being in a violent domestic situation made me feel that I needed to take these steps to protect myself, perhaps it was time to exit the marriage before. I didn't want my life nor my daughter's to be thrust into a negative situation because rage, anger or fear ignited.

CHAPTER 12
THE LANDSCAPE OF MARRIAGE

Nia's birth was my most beautiful experience. She was perfect. Holding a tiny six pounds eleven ounce baby girl in my arms that stretched twenty-one inches long let me know what I'd demand out of life. From that moment on, I would spend my life keeping her safe and working as hard as I could to make sure she never wanted for anything, especially love. I didn't know where Cedric and I would end up, but I wanted to try and make it work. I wanted a family, but I didn't want Nia to grow up with a broken family. I wanted her to live a happy and whole life with both parents present and loving her as much as possible.

After my physical scars diminished, things returned to normal. I never spoke about that abusive situation because I thought it was the only way to move forward in our marriage. I was ashamed and I couldn't logically make any excuses for Cedric. I wasn't able to explain why he sat on my stomach while I was nearly seven months pregnant. There was no justification for the abuse I withstood or his excuses. Part of me wanted to let it go as if it never happened, but it was embedded deeply inside of me. The fact that I was carrying his child didn't protect me from his outrages so it was evident our relationship was dysfunctional at that point. The thought of being alone, while pregnant, induced fear. At that moment in time, I really didn't know what to do. Instead of removing myself from an unhealthy environment, I thought about having to change all of my insurance beneficiary documents, my name back to my maiden name and explain the situation to my employer. If I left at that time, I would have had to explain to Nia why her father wasn't around and why I was divorced. I would have failed at our marriage and the commitment we made. It would have been easy for Cedric to dismiss the short-lived relationship as just another bad one and move on to the next. I believed that I was supposed to be a good wife and stand by my husband regardless of whatever came.

    I tried to put myself in my husband's shoes and consider what he was going through. He was in the process of building his contracting business and it was difficult for him to find good, dependable employees. Eventually, he found a couple of solid workers and was able to devote more time at home. He stayed home for the first six months after Nia's birth and took care of her. He changed diapers, did laundry, cooked and played with her in the most loving way. I went back to work after exhausting eight weeks of maternity leave and Cedric became a stay-at-home Dad. Nia loved the attention from his cuddling and nurturing and I loved watching their interaction together. I thought this experience as a dad and his time with her would change him for the better. He had an undeniable natural instinct with children. He knew when she was hungry or irritable and stayed by her side to make sure she had everything she needed. Nia was a beautiful, healthy and happy little baby, which reassured me that I made the right decision.

When Cedric went back to work after caring for Nia full-time, he claimed that being a stay-at-home Dad was difficult and challenging for him because he was accustom to working every day. At the time, I thought he was doing an excellent job with our daughter. It wasn't until much later that I realized he was uncomfortable with our role reversal. He revealed that he felt less of a man when he stayed home as a caregiver. When Nia was six months old, she began daycare and Cedric returned to work. Our routine changed drastically. We had to adjust our schedules and coordinate dropping off and picking Nia up from the daycare center. Even with both of us working tirelessly, we committed to making Nia a priority.

The pattern of abuse became evident on January 28, 2001. I could never allow Nia to witness me being touched by Cedric in a way that required calling the police. As a parent and a woman, it is not acceptable to allow children to witness physical or verbal abuse between parents.

Our house had an eerie silence circulating. After the police officers took my husband, I hugged Nia for a long time. We sat quietly, trying to make sense of everything that transpired.

"Mom, I was scared and I didn't know what to do," was all that Nia said. Her little eyes were filled with a look I never wanted to see again.

My eyes were full of tears and my voice was shaky as I responded, "Don't ever let a man put his hands on you if it's not in a loving manner." That was a devastating moment. The situation was bad enough between Cedric and I but I couldn't allow Nia to think this was acceptable. I didn't want my daughter's mindset to be shaped with that negative and dysfunctional image of marriage or a relationship.

Nia still had her pajamas on so I told her to shower and get dressed. It was around one-thirty that afternoon. While she showered, I went upstairs into our bedroom and sat in the green terry cloth and comfort chair in the corner of our bedroom. It was the type of chair that totally consumed you and that's what I needed at the moment. As I glanced around the bedroom, I noticed our bed was still unmade and Cedric's brown slippers sat against the wall. His sock drawer was open. His keys, cufflinks, polo cologne and the Zemis carving we bought during our visit to Jamaica sat on top of the dresser. Everything appeared normal, but it wasn't. I knew that I could not stay in this marriage. I covered my face with my hands and felt the dark reality of my marriage rising up from inside of me. What do I tell Nia? How do I begin the process of ending my marriage? How did I let this happen? This isn't how a marriage should be. I needed the marriage more than Cedric wanted me and that wasn't love. I thought I knew all the answers to making it work. It shattered my heart that Nia was present when all control was lost. Hiding my black eyes, making excuses and terrified that another abusive episode would ensue was no way to live. I really wanted to pray for the answers, but I let an eruption of heaviness breech my physical being and pour out like a torrential rainfall. I began to count the times Cedric put his hands on me. When my adrenaline settled down, all I felt was exhaustion. Tears streamed down my cheeks and continued to flow. I couldn't stop crying. That night faded to black.

I knew that this type of relationship wasn't conducive to Nia or me. I forgave Cedric and he went to counseling for his anger. Two years passed since the 911 incident and we were still together. There weren't any other incidents until Easter Sunday in 2003 when we were driving home from church. Cedric and I were in the front and Nia was in the back seat. We were talking about Cedric's driving tactics and ended up arguing about it. He started waving his hand in front of my face and screamed that he'd do anything he wanted to me and dared me to call the police. I think it was at this moment, I knew he felt invincible and I needed to end the marriage. The argument didn't escalate any further, but I was tired of feeling threatened. I began taking steps towards a divorce and made Cedric aware of my decision and why. He said he wasn't going anywhere, meaning he wasn't going to make it easy. Regardless, I no longer tolerated the life I was living and the example I was setting for Nia. I was tired of walking on eggshells and being fearful of his tone and mood swings. As much as I loved him, I didn't like the man he had become and I couldn't stand to look in the mirror and see the woman I'd been reduced to. I'd waited too long for change and if I didn't make it at that point, it may not have happened.

On July 2, 2003 Nia went to Girl Scouts camp. She was scheduled to be up North for camping, crafts, swimming and horseback riding with her fellow Brownie Troops. The event lasted for four days. In a deliberate action, I arranged for Cedric to be served an Emergency Order of Protection along with a Petition for Divorce from the First Judicial District Family Court Division during this time. The police came to the house, served him the papers, asked Cedric to pack his personal belongings and escorted him out of the house. When I came home from work, he was gone, his truck was gone and so was a part of me. I knew it was the right thing to do. Actually, it was the best thing to do and I had prolonged the inevitable. It was time to regain my happiness. Although the process wasn't easy, my divorce was a much-needed progression towards becoming whole again.

Despite being able to document a pattern of physical abuse and get the court to grant an Order of Protection, it wasn't adequate enough in family court, in the case of dissolution of marriage. The goal of the judge was to ensure that both parties walk away with a reasonable amount of assets when he released the husband and wife from all matrimonial obligations. The fact that someone was abusive does not factor in. Divorce is about finances and splitting assets. In the end, it seems like you are dissolving a business matter more than a marriage.

Divorce is difficult regardless of the situations that occurred or final outcome because the marriage began with love. It is financially and emotionally draining. It is a union protected by the judicial system and created by God. So, when you marry, do your research and understand who it is that you are marrying. There are warning signs and indicators that reveal the type of individual he or she is. The problem we make is that we choose to ignore the signs. If you are in an abusive marriage or relationship, make a plan to leave. Prepare yourself for the financial strains because they're inevitable, but don't allow it to be the reason you stay in an abusive or loveless marriage. If you have children, give serious thought to what they are learning and how you are allowing it to shape their mind. We wonder how children end up becoming abusers or how young women allow it, but it is a learned behavior that we must end. We must not use violence as a means to discipline.

During my divorce, the judge split our assets, bills and obligations down the middle. It took me eight years to completely pay off all financial obligations once my divorce was finalized, but it was worth it.

I got rid of my Lipstick Allí box and no longer kept the secrets. Going through a divorce exposed everything that was vital during our marriage. The judge had no idea what I really went through during the course of our marriage. It is important to assess all areas of the relationship before you become emotionally involved. Look into someone's history a little closer without being so quick to dismiss the signs or negative patterns. Just remember that love doesn't hurt.

I returned to my life learning to protect myself from harm by investing in getting to know people instead of focusing on what I want to see. Unless we take the time to make the right decisions and walk away from anyone that threatens our peace and wellbeing, you too may end up living in the black. Black eyes, black and blue bruises and black sunglasses to shield the shame is not the way you want to live. Seek help before the option fades from your mind. Want more for yourself and your children.

TIDBITS
As long as you believe in your dreams, your journey will be relevant.

ABOUT THE AUTHORS

Brenda Blackmon is a sales leader in the pharmaceutical industry with a Bachelor of Arts degree from the University of Minnesota. She is a mother and currently resides in Kansas City. She loves to golf, play the piano, travel and enjoy life. She shares her perspective on life on twitter with tidbits of tough love and inspiration. Join her on twitter @bbluvu20 and share your thoughts. For more information visit www.brenda-blackmon.com.

Alyssa Curry is a young woman illuminated by her passion for life. She has a Bachelor of Science in the field of Psychology. Alyssa is an award-winning novelist, book cover, graphic designer and copyeditor that spends her free time engulfed in music. For design or ghostwriting services, contact her at alyssa@seraphbooks.com.

www.ingramcontent.com/pod-product-compliance
Lightning Source LLC
Chambersburg PA
CBHW022110090426
42743CB00008B/794